AF215144

Mindful Judaism
A Jewish Guide to Beating Stress and Anxiety
By
Marvin Shaw
ISBN: 978-1-9997156-4-9

Published by

PUBLISHING

i2i Publishing. Manchester
www.i2ipublishing.co.uk

CONTENTS

5

FOREWORDS (1)

Marvin is an accomplished, experienced and talented author having written many inspiring and thought-provoking books. This book is no exception to the trend already set by Marvin.

Mindful Judaism is an exceptional and fascinating guide to living a happy and fulfilled Jewish life. It assists the reader to not only improve their middos (character traits) as he/she navigates through life's challenges, trials and tribulations but it also enables the reader to feel a deeper and closer spiritual connection to G-d.

Mindful Judaism highlights the unique gift of life, that everyone is special, each with their own G-d given mission in life. The book provides each and every one of us with the tools to be able to fulfil our mission in life by examining in detail the twelve most important characteristics of our divine soul. The book reminds us that G-d has actually given us the skills to deal with life's challenges. The book guides us how to develop and enhance those skills. It stresses the importance of maintaining a balance in our relationships and lives.

Everyone who reads this book will gain considerably and will be sure to improve their quality of life.

I highly recommend it.

Reverend David Kale L.L.B. (Hons) L'Pool
Minister Staines and District United Synagogue

FOREWORDS (2)

Marvin has done it again! Another epic masterpiece, deftly put together and even more comprehensive than his previous classic works.

From Kaballah to Kelm, the author delves into sources far and wide in his quest to enlighten the reader (in his delightful and easy reading style) with the key to *Mindful Judaism.*

If you've picked up this volume, you can do a lot worse than read it.

Buy it now - but beware - you won't put it down for a while. Sheer magnetism!

Well, what are you waiting for - get started, and be mindful about it!

Rabbi Mashiach Kelaty - Stanmore Sephardi Congregation

FOREWORDS (3)

Marvin Shaw's mission is to help those who are in trouble, those who see the world as broken and chaotic. His gentle, non-judgmental toolkit for Mindfulness brings a uniquely Jewish perspective to this puzzle of how to heal, calm and and order lives that have gone out of control. Using an eclectic mix of psalms, teachings, visualisation techniques and the framework of the Jewish year, his book has something to offer everyone. Shaw's voice is always one of sweetness and kindness.

Maureen Kendler (*London School of Jewish Studies Teaching Fellow*)

ACKNOWLEDGEMENTS AND SOURCES

I am both delighted and amazed – in equal measure – to be able to present my fifth book to you.

There are so many people to thank – without whose contribution this work would not have been possible.

I would thus like to give thanks and appreciation to the following authors, notable people and websites. Please note that I have not referenced, here, my century old sources.

My wonderful **sources** include (in no particular order):

Alan Morinis - *Founder and Dean of the Mussar Institute (also author of several books and articles)*

Osher Chaim Levene and Yehoshua Hartman - *Jewish Wisdom in the Numbers*

Rabbi Zelig Pliskin - *Growth through Tehillim*

Christopher Andre - *25 Ways to Live in the Moment through Art*

Elisha Goldstein - *Uncovering Happiness*

Avraham Yaakov Finkel - *Kabbalah*

Rabbi Akiva Tatz - *Letters to a Buddhist Jew*

Rabbi Yitzchak Shochet - *Rabbi of Mill Hill United Synagogue*

Rabbi Samuel Landau - *Rabbi of Kingston, Surbiton and District United Synagogue*

Rabbi David Roberts – *Rabbi of Kehillas Netzach Yisroel*

Frumma Rosenberg Gottleib - *Chabad.org*

Rabbi Tali Loewenthal - *Chabad.org*

Rabbi Tsvi Freeman - *Chabad.org*

Nachum Mohl - *Jewishmag.com*

Rabbi Yitzchak Ginsberg - *Inner.org*

Aish.com

Jewishpathways.com

Samantha Brick – *Stella Magazine*

Rabbi Shlomo Wolbe

Rabbi Eliyahu Dessler

Rabbi Leib Chasman

Rabbi Yechezkel Levenstein

Rabbi Eliyahu Lopian

Rabbi David Katz

Rabbi Danny Kirsch

Rabbi Ivan Ziskind

Rabbi Yitzchak Sandler

Viktor Frankl

Rabbi Lord Jonathan Sacks

Lubavitcher Rebbe - Rabbi Menachem M. Schneerson

I would especially like to give an extra-special thanks to:

Maureen Kendler (London School of Jewish Studies Teaching Fellow), Rabbi Mashiach Kelaty and Reverend David Kale (Minister of Staines and District United Synagogue) for their delightful and inspiring forewords

Adele Rendel, for her magnificent mindful front cover painting and her artwork throughout the book

Lionel Ross www.i2ipublishing.co.uk (proprietor & publisher) for his wise advice and incredible patience. This is the fourth book of mine he has published! Also, thank you to his designer Dino Caruana for his sterling work

Barry Alan Shaw (brother and photographic wizard) for his back-cover photo

My mum Rita (Rachel) Shaw for her everlasting love, friendship and support

My caring and loving late dad Eddie Shaw who I'll always miss and love in equal amounts

Finally, I thank G-d for giving me the gifts and circumstances that have allowed this book to be conceived and written.

I bless all my readers and their families with good health, happiness and joy and the mindful vision to always be aware of this wonderful world in which we live.

Shalom
Marvin J Shaw
Elul 5777

Painting on the book-cover and illustrations throughout the book created by Adele Rendel

INTRODUCTION

Can appearances can be deceptive?

We naturally like to feel that our lives are a success; that they have value and meaning and that we are striding purposefully forward towards becoming enlightened beings.

Yet, if the truth be told, we often sense that something is missing and we may feel somewhat disappointed with our lives. This feeling may only be fleeting or it may occur more frequently. It may be something to do with our relationships, employment or spirituality. Or it could be connected to our health, our desired legacy or our mortality. Perhaps we feel that we are not realising our true potential. We may not even know what is lacking – just a sense that things are not the way they are meant to be.

Yet, even if we have some intellectual understanding of the way forward, that special knowledge often has not seeped down into our hearts, our souls and our emotions.

Yes, we may know that we are children of G-d, our Creator and thus should be feeling full of self-esteem and unbounded joy.

Yet, even if we don't, we can be comforted by the words of Rabbi Yisrael Salanter - the founder of the *Mussar* movement - who says:

"As long as one lives a life of calmness and tranquillity in the service of G-d...he is remote from true service." (See more in Chapter Four – Equanimity)

In this book, I focus on twelve soul-traits that can transform our lives - of which equanimity is just one. I am greatly indebted to the detailed work and research that Alan Morinis, founder and Dean of The Mussar Institute, has put into this subject and I shall quote often from his books. Yet I hope that I take forward his work to an exciting new plateau by including my own and others' particular perspectives.

How do we decide which of the twelve soul-traits we need to work on at any one time? Alan Morinis advises that:

'Where we feel or cause pain is a big clue, because, since we tend to be creatures of habit, our most important *behira* points (moments of free-choice where we are unsure of what to do) are often associated with repeated problems, and they are usually problems that bring suffering to ourselves and to others.'

We may, for example, feel consistently frustrated over the poor service of utilities companies. It is often difficult to get to speak to anyone on the phone these days – let alone someone who can actually deal well with our problem. The long waits we sometimes have to endure may annoy even the most mild-mannered of people.

The soul-traits I think we'd need to focus on, in this instance, are *equanimity* (see Chapter Four) and *patience* (see Chapter Ten). Equanimity is accepting that everything will not always be as we would wish it to be; whereas having patience with someone means that we are able to deal with them in a calm but assertive way.

Alan Morinis (on jewishpathways.com) indicates the importance of mastering the soul-traits. He quotes Chaim

Vital (an associate of the famous 16th century kabbalist the *Ari):*

'The 16th century kabbalist, Rabbi Chaim Vital, explains in *Sha'arey Kedusha 1:2:*

"The inner traits were not included in the 613 *mitzvot* (commandments), yet they are integral to them since they are a prerequisite to the *mitzvot* themselves. Therefore, the one who possesses inferior inner traits is worse off than one who is only committing transgressions. Since the inner traits are such an important foundation, they were not included in the *mitzvot*. Good inner traits lead to *mitzvot*. One should be more concerned about his inner traits than *his mitzvot*."'

(I have also read an article by the well-respected rabbi and author Rabbi Abraham Twerski saying precisely the same thing).

Morinis advises that we study the soul-traits, meditate on them, chant them with great passion (e.g. when reciting "patience is a virtue") and journal about them extensively.

I hope that you enjoy reading this fifth book of mine on well-being and self-improvement and I bless you with success in becoming the very best person you can truly be.

Let's now get to work on acquiring these twelve important soul-traits right away; so we can bring them to the fore whenever we need their desirable and life-enhancing qualities.

DEFINING MINDFUL JUDAISM

What is *Mindful Judaism?*

It is not, let me say from the outset, anything to do with Buddhism. I appreciate that mindfulness has its roots in that religion - yet *Mindful Judaism* isn't exactly identical to mindfulness either.

So what is it then?

It is primarily about living in the present and appreciating the present in a Jewish context.

Let me explain.

I remember well, being on a bus at the Dead Sea. There had been heavy rains in Jerusalem that day, and the waters had rolled all the way down the hills to Dead Sea level. This led to so much flooding that the bus had to come to a halt in its journey. Yet the view was both beautiful and memorable. It was not raining, but sunny with blue skies instead. So I took my leave temporarily from the stranded bus to experience this memorable scene of flood waters, in the biblical land of Israel. They reached nearly up to my knees. Naturally I wanted to photograph such a rare sight. Just one problem, though. I didn't have my camera with me!

I resolved, then and there, to take a mental photo instead. I blinked my eyes and the scene became indelibly marked on my memory – making the actual moment much more powerful than a thousand photos ever could.

Often, taking photos can actually detract from our experience. We are so busy with trying to take the perfect picture, that the event or place passes us by. *Mindful Judaism* is about appreciating each moment in life at the time it happens; taking one moment and one day at a time.

Judaism places great stock in us being thankful to others and G-d (see Chapter Eleven – Gratitude). Unlike Buddhism, it is also about engaging with (not escaping from) the world. It is especially about making each moment holy and meaningful. That is why Jews say so many blessings. These are there to enable us to give thanks to G-d for all the gifts He gives us. They are opportunities for us to show appreciation to G-d for life - the greatest gift of all. Moreover, by saying a blessing, we make our actions holy.

To explore further, let us see what Rabbi Samuel Landau has to say about mindfulness as it relates to Judaism (as reported in the Jewish Chronicle of October 8th 2015):

'As a clinical psychologist in training, I often use (mindfulness) meditations with my patients and am investigating mindfulness for my doctoral thesis. Mindfulness originated as a Buddhist meditative practice but was secularised and applied in the West by Jon Kabat-Zin (a Jew of course).

Mindfulness has become ubiquitous; helping people live with the distress of both physical and mental health conditions, deal with stress in the workplace, manage challenges at school, and more. It almost seems that wherever one seeks an answer to life's difficulties, mindfulness is presented as a possible answer. Does Judaism have an analogue (something comparable)?

In the episode of perhaps the most dramatic *Torah* (biblical) reading of the High Holy Days period – that of the *Akedah*, the binding of Isaac - a word is used, a word that appears in the entire *Torah* only a handful of times; "*Hineini*", "Here I am". In Genesis 22, God calls to Abraham, a call that would herald Abraham's final and most difficult test: "Sacrifice your son to Me." Abraham responds humbly and with readiness*: "Hineini."*

Abraham does not simply grunt in assent or acknowledge the Caller. Rather, he seems to understand that this interaction with the Divine will require a certain mode of being, a mindful mode. Abraham must accept that all the yearning of long, childless years along with the laughing joy of Isaac's birth must accompany him on this test. All the anxieties of dashed hopes for a monotheistic successor would climb the mountain with him. And yet if he were lost in these thoughts, he would not complete the test. And so Abraham answers "*Hineini*" - Here I am, in my totality, in the present moment, non-judgmentally accepting my experience, my test, feeling the climb.

The *Akedah* passage may suggest that a mindful or *Hineini* approach is part of the Jewish experience; a way to engage one's essence meaningfully with the trials and tribulations that God presents us.

Yet how do we square our Jewish sensitivities with a practice that is built on Buddhism, even in its Kabat-Zinn incarnation? Can we still use it to achieve the heights of *Hineini?* To my mind, the answer has to do with our approach; if we consider mindfulness to be an end in itself, a state of being that is simply more beneficial for wellbeing, we may have missed an opportunity. After all, Judaism has a strong focus on doing rather than just being. Rather, mindfulness meditation should serve as a means to an end, the end being a deeper engagement with our Jewish journey, making mindfulness a welcome addition to a Jewish life's toolbox.

(Samuel Landau is rabbi of Kingston, Surbiton and District United Synagogue)

Frumma Rosenberg-Gottlieb on chabad.org similarly wonders if mindfulness is compatible with Judaism:

'Is mindfulness, I wondered, an ingredient in a *Torah* life? I rarely heard my *Torah* teachers speak of cultivating inner awareness. Over time, however, as I became more sophisticated in my understanding of *Torah* (Jewish law and teachings), I realised that mindfulness and a peaceful, balanced soul is indeed an objective in Jewish life, and that the tools for attaining it are subtly woven into the tapestry of *Torah* knowledge. I learned, for example, that the Hebrew word *"shalom"* implies not just peace, but also completion, perfection, wholeness.

We bless one another with peace; our daily prayers culminate in a request for peace.......Chassidic philosophy demonstrates how inner turmoil is reduced when we have a clear understanding of our goals, and how the cultivation of trust, faith, awareness, and freedom from doubt enriches our life with joy. I began to discover that Jewish tradition deeply addresses topics that many of us first encountered in other ancient cultures, or in practices and perspectives currently referred to as "New Age."

Commentaries on the life of Abraham suggest that when he sent his offspring to the East bearing gifts, these gifts included aspects of meditative practices that eventually surfaced in Far Asian spiritual teachings. Some speculate that a Hindu caste of holy men is called "Brahmans" after the Abrahamic tradition that spawned them. Abraham's son Isaac was a meditator; when his bride Rebecca first saw him, he was "meditating in the fields" — and the Biblical accounts of his practice of "digging wells" are understood to signify his delving into the depths of consciousness.

Many of the early holy men in Jewish history were shepherds who chose the pastoral lifestyle in order to be able to meditate in the fields. Talmudic sages and mystical Kabbalists had a longstanding tradition to meditate before and during prayer; since the time of the Baal Shem Tov, *chassidim* have carried this legacy forward until the current day.....

Meditation is a balm to the soul, an antidote to anxiety, a channel to the understanding of G-d's greatness — and man's insignificance. At the same time, it also empowers and imbues us with Divine energy.

There are many forms of meditation, beginning with simple relaxation exercises involving attention to the breath or other bodily sensations. Other elementary techniques employ a word or phrase, repeated mentally in order to elicit a relaxation response and transcendent thought. Guided imagery (visualisation) allows the imagination to experience beauty and tranquillity — because to the subconscious mind, imagination and reality are the same. The *chassidic* practice of *hitbonenut* meditation involves actively contemplating a spiritual concept until it expands our creative intelligence, deepens our awareness, and becomes an indelible part of our consciousness.

Prayer is an advanced form of meditation; yet it is also simple and accessible to all. The Hebrew word for prayer, *tefillah*, implies connecting to and bonding with one's spiritual source. In fact the prayer-book, the *siddur*, can be seen as a highly sophisticated, structured guide to cultivating our awareness of the presence and the power of G-d.

Mindfulness naturally enhances a person's sense of being present in the moment, rather than anxious about the future or stuck in the unhappy past. Even a brief beginner's experience of "being in the now" is uplifting and refreshing. When we are able to string such moments together and become more mindful over a sustained period of time, a remarkable transformation of consciousness begins to emerge. We begin to become aware of what the Kabbalists and Chassidic masters refer to as "continuous creation" — how G-d, in His benevolence, creates the universe anew each moment. This in turn empowers us to recognize our own newness from moment to moment, so that we are not only disencumbered from whatever negativity we may have experienced before, but we are free to collaborate, so to speak, with the power of Divine creativity in manifesting a new and improved world.

In the past hundred years or so, quantum physicists have begun to discover and explore the deep conceptual basis of this liberating perspective; more recently, New Age gurus have learned how to capitalise on the idea. From a *Torah* perspective, this has been known for many centuries as the art of cultivating *bitachon*, trust (see Chapter Eight).'

I write this in the middle of the *Omer* period when we count the forty-nine days between the Jewish festivals of *Pesach* and *Shavuot*. I heard Rabbi Danny Kirsch from London's JLE say, only yesterday, that as we count each day (e.g. this is the sixteenth day of the *Omer* that is two weeks and two days) we should appreciate that **on this unique day** we have special opportunities for growth and *mitzvot* that will never repeat themselves. In other words - that the Counting of the Omer reminds us of the once-in-a-lifetime gift of each and every unique day of our lives.

Appreciating and living this gift is what *Mindful Judaism* is all about. It is achieved by working on the twelve soul-traits described in depth in this book…..in a mindful way.

Like Judaism, it is all about balance. So, yes, we should be patient (see Chapter Ten), for example, but not forever. We need to get a move on and get things done too.

Similarly, we must have order and structure in our lives (see Chapter Two) - but also creativity and spontaneity.

Just as *Shabbat* (the Jewish Sabbath) and the Jewish festivals are welcome stopping-off points for reflection, rest, enjoyment and study - we also need to be active and engaged with the rest of the week and year. *Mindful Judaism* reminds and encourages us to maintain balance in our relationships and lives.

So let us take time to meditate on nature and beautiful paintings. Then let us make the most of any learning or insights we have experienced - and take action for the good of all.

Let us also read poetry. Then, let us write some of our own; or keep a journal of our thoughts, actions and feelings. As the late singer-songwriter Harry Chapin wrote in his fourteen minute opus *There Only Was One Choice:*

'Just write about your feelings...not the things you never did.'

Or, to quote King Solomon from Proverbs 12:25:

'Worry in man's heart should be talked out'

So let us talk about our feelings as well as write about them.

Let us also do *mitzvot* (good things) to other people – whilst taking some time out for ourselves, too.

Let us embrace and immerse ourselves in the beautiful Jewish festivals and concepts that we have. Let us study and pray but let us also enjoy good food and rest.

Everything is in the *Torah* (Jewish teachings). Whether our interest is science or art, psychology or nature......we will discover it in Judaism.

Finding our passion in life and in our particular interests in the *Torah*.....Living our life to the utmost and being the best person we can be.....Appreciating each moment of our lives and thanking G-d for the gift of life.....that is *Mindful Judaism.*

WHAT MUSSAR IS – AND HOW IT CAN TRANSFORM OUR LIVES

'*Mussar* is a Jewish spiritual tradition that offers insight and guidance for living - by directing us to pay attention to the impact that our inner traits have on our lives. The *Mussar* teachers take note of the *Torah's* teaching, "You shall be holy" (Leviticus 19:1), and find in this injunction the primary guidance for living. They perceive that each of us at our core is inherently a holy being, and the issue of living is to recognise and then to remove the obstacles to that inborn holiness.

Those obstacles show up in our lives as inner traits *(middot)* that are tending toward either extreme. Those extreme qualities (which will be different for each of us) make up a personal spiritual curriculum, whether that be too much or too little patience, an excessive tendency to generosity or miserliness, rage or indifference, and so on. The path of *Mussar* begins with coming to awareness of the traits that are on your spiritual curriculum, and then doing the work to change those traits, to bring them back toward the mean.

(For example) a person who is easily and often angered counts rage on their spiritual curriculum, just as the habitually stingy person has been assigned to master generosity. The impatient person has patience on his or her curriculum, and the worried person has been given an assignment to develop trust.

When the impatient person becomes patient, or the harsh person masters kindness, or the lazy one becomes energetic, then a spiritual obstacle is lifted, and more of the light of holiness shines brightly into that person's life and, through them, into the world. Each trait that is mastered in this way brings you one step closer to being whole: *shalem:* and to knowing peace: *shalom.*

Mussar is not "self-help." Its purpose is not so you will gratify all your desires, but so that you will become the master of your desires, in order that you can fulfil your potential, which is spiritual above all else.

As Rabbi Yechezkel Levenstein, a recent *Mussar* teacher put it, "A person's primary mission in this world is to purify and elevate his soul"'

Alan Morinis

In this book, I have chosen twelve optimum soul-traits from a long list that Morinis includes in his books. These have specifically been selected as they correspond to the twelve Jewish months of the year. Each Jewish month contains special energies and offers personal growth opportunities that are connected to the month in question. This will be illustrated as we progress through the book. (For more detailed analysis, see my book *Kosher Happiness*).

In this book, I give a full explanation of each particular trait, so that you will understand exactly what working on that soul-trait involves. I also include a phrase (at the beginning of each chapter) that captures the essence of what that trait is about. Alan Morinis uses different phrases to me and you may decide to choose phrases that, for you, best encompass what each soul-trait means to you.

Morinis describes how these phrases can be utilised:

'The phrase that accompanies each trait is meant to capture the essence of that trait in words. You are given these phrases in order to set up a daily morning contemplation of the trait, so that you start your day with that day's trait firmly embedded in your consciousness. The simplest way to do this contemplation is to repeat the phrase to yourself several times. Better still is to repeat it aloud. In the nineteenth century, the practice was to repeat the phrase over and over, chanting it with a melody and allowing the heart to soar with emotion. (This is the traditional *Mussar* practice known as *hitpa'alut*, which is often translated as "chanting with lips aflame.")

Contemplating the daily phrase raises your awareness of the day's trait. You will be amazed at the effect that extra awareness has. Not only will you see that particular trait so much more clearly as it shows up in your day, you will also be much more aware of how you yourself embody that trait, and the choices you have in how you express it.'

LOVING OURSELVES AND OTHERS

Judaism's most famous commandment is to *love your neighbour as yourself* (Leviticus 19:18). I think that sometimes we forget the 'as yourself' part. Yet actually, the above statement concludes with *I am Hashem (G-d)*; thus, it is saying, we should love our neighbour, ourselves and G-d – because that is what G-d commands of us.

I heard Rabbi Danny Kirsch (who runs London's JLE) talk about 'love' just the other day. He was speaking prior to the minor Jewish festival of *Tu B'Av,* sometimes colloquially known as 'Jewish Valentine's Day.'

He told the story of a man who went to a therapist to help him sort out a personal problem. The therapist advised him to go for a walk for twenty minutes, first of all, in order to put himself in a calm state of mind.

The man went out, but walked for just five minutes; then, feeling he was now ready, returned to the therapist.

The therapist rebuked him and said "Why have you returned so soon? I told you to walk for twenty minutes. You must have met someone you hated - and thus returned early."

"You are wrong. I didn't meet anyone" the client blurted out in righteous indignation.

"Yes you did" the therapist responded. "You met YOURSELF!"

We may not actually hate ourselves; but, as the story indicates, it is indeed sometimes difficult for us to enjoy and to bear our own company.

Yes, we need to be able to love G-d and our neighbour; but in this day and age, it seems that the hardest person to learn to love and be with - is ourselves.

It is not a matter of self-love in the narcissistic way that we are talking about here. Instead, it is the vital matter of feeling good about ourselves; happy in and with ourselves. So that we are then able to love others - and have enough confidence and self-esteem - in order to do good and be a blessing to the world.

The Maharal of Prague (one of the outstanding Jewish minds of the sixteenth century) tells us that 'love of all creatures is also love of G-d, for whoever loves the One loves all the works that He has made.' This being so (adds the Alter of Slabodka) we must love not only the unfortunate and tormented, but even the well-fed and the haughty.

The biggest secret of all, according to Rabbi Dessler, is that 'love is a consequence of giving. When a person gives, it is as if he is giving part of himself. He therefore loves the recipient because he finds in him something of himself.....he will (thus) find himself included in the other. Then he can (literally) love his neighbour - as himself.'

I am indebted to Alan Morinis for the above quotes from his book *Every Day Holy Day*. Alan, himself, explains that love means that we are no longer separate from the other which is why losing someone or something we love hurts so much.

Thus when we lose someone we love, a part of ourselves is torn away.

The *Mindful Judaism* way to achieve love is to work through the twelve soul-traits in a way that puts the focus on loving and feeling at peace with ourselves, others, G-d and the world around us. In order to facilitate this, I have added, in each chapter, a section about how the trait we are focusing on connects with love. This will, in turn, also deepen our understanding of the value of the particular trait in question.

Love, I can reveal, is the 'hidden' thirteenth soul-trait. The number thirteen is, interestingly enough, an auspicious number in Judaism. In a Jewish leap year (which happens seven times in a nineteen-year period) there are thirteen months in that year. The month that is added is a second month of *Adar* - the happiest month in the Jewish year - in which the festival of *Purim* falls. On *Purim* we dress in costume - and it has many aspects of hiddenness connected to it. Notably, it is also known as the festival when the Jewish people accepted the *Torah* (Jewish Law) with **love**. (This is opposed to *Shavuot* when some of our teachings say that we accepted the *Torah* under duress – literally with G-d holding a mountain over our head).

The (thirteenth) leap year month is called *Adar Sheni* which means second *Adar*. This is the specific month in which - in leap years - the joyous festival of *Purim* is celebrated.

It is interesting to note that the words 'one' *(echod)* and 'love' *(ahava)* both have the *gematria* (Jewish numerical equivalent) of thirteen. Combined, they add up to twenty-six, the numerical value of G-d's name (of mercy) *Hashem*. My blessing is that we all experience much love and oneness in our lives.

MINDFUL JUDAISM AND THE NUMBERS

When I picked the 12 soul-traits for this book, it was not a random exercise. It was a personal and specific selection taken from a list of soul-traits in Alan Morinis's excellent book *Everyday Holiness*.

The soul-traits I chose were those that I found to be most necessary and worthy for us to live a happy and fulfilled life. However, as I mention above (when discussing *mussar*), I also had in mind their connection to the special energies *(hooshim)* - and opportunities to grow - that are present in each of the 12 months of the Jewish year. These are detailed in depth in my book *Kosher Happiness.*

Thus the first soul-trait of faith *(emunah)* connects to the first month of the Jewish year. That month is *Nissan* which contains the major festival of *Pesach* (Passover) when the Jewish people showed tremendous *faith* in G-d as they escaped Egypt after two hundred and ten years of slavery. A prime example of this is when Nachshon Ben Aminadav (from the tribe of Judah) was bold and believing enough up to go up to his neck into the Reed Sea, before the waters eventually parted. (The tribe of Judah is notably connected to *Nissan* - see *Kosher Happiness.)*

Similarly, the eighth soul-trait, which is trust *(bitachon)* connects to the properties of the eighth month of the Jewish year - *Cheshvan* - and so on.

It is fascinating how all similar classifications in Judaism connect. This indicates that the number 1 connects to the first month *Nissan* and to the first soul-trait of 'faith'. Just as the number 8 must be aligned with the eighth month of the Jewish year, *Cheshvan,* and the eighth soul-trait of 'trust.'

In each chapter, I have thus explored this exciting connection between the numbers and their respective soul-traits (with the help of the illuminating book *Jewish Wisdom in the Numbers* by Osher Chaim Levene and Rabbi Yehoshua Hartman). This again deepens our understanding and appreciation of each soul-trait.

EXPERIENCING MINDFUL JUDAISM

In order for you to experience the soul-traits, I have included in each chapter a poem (written by me) and verses from one of King David's Psalms.

These have been specially chosen to relate to whichever soul-trait you happen to be working on at any one time. The benefits of reading poetry and psalms aloud are illustrated in depth in my books *Poetry for Health* and *Modern Day Psalms.*

Suffice it to say that by reciting these verses with real understanding and expression, you will become at one with each soul-trait and allow their unique essence to affect your emotions in a positive way.

Similarly the *mindful visualisation for healing*, listed after the *psalm* section of each chapter, will enhance your experience of the soul-trait you are studying and also aid relaxation.

On a more intellectual (mind) level, the *inner secret* segment in each chapter will further deepen your understanding and fascination of all twelve soul-traits – as well as giving practical tips of how to access them more easily.

PUTTING IT INTO PRACTICE

There are various ways to put *Mindful Judaism* into practice.

Firstly let us look at the methods of meditation *(hitbonenut)*, retreat in silence *(hitbodedut)* and diary practices *(chesbon hanefesh)*.

MEDITATION

The meditation *(hitbonenut)* is normally done by focusing on a simple word or phrase. Thus, at the beginning of each chapter, I have included a suggested phrase for you to repeat. The idea being that by repeating the phrase (for the particular soul-trait you are working on) makes its essence becomes second nature to you. Of course, if you prefer to construct and utilise another phrase that is more meaningful to you – then please do so.

For example, the suggested phrase in Chapter One is "My faith creates a life of meaning." You may choose (for short) to repeat the word "faith" instead.

RETREAT IN SILENCE

Now let us examine the practice of retreat in silence. Rabbi Shlomo Wolbe comments on its benefits:

'You only get a feeling for your internal life when you are alone. With a half hour of being alone you can come to feel things you never knew about yourself - and see what you are lacking in spirituality. You will set new goals to reach.

This can only be done if you spend time alone in seclusion *(hitbodedut)* for a half hour. In this way you can start to build your internal, spiritual world.'

My own preference is to do this whilst strolling in nature or when walking home from my mum's after a Friday night *Shabbat* (Sabbath) meal.

DIARY PRACTICES

I also like the idea of diary practices such as writing a 'stream of consciousness' diary. This is a private journal in which you can write down anything that is on your mind. This firstly allows you to get any worries you may have off your chest.

As you continue to let your writing flow, it then generally flows into a source of creative ideas or a fount of deep seated desires. I find this to be a very valuable exercise and would encourage you to give it a try. (For more on the benefits of writing, please see my book *Poetry for Health*). The important thing is to write whatever comes into your head - and to keep writing for a number of minutes. Remember, this journal is for you and for you alone to see.

Another, more formal, way to use the beneficial practice of writing is to keep a regular diary. Reflecting on the events of the day, in relation to how well (or otherwise) we have progressed with the particular soul-trait/s we are working with, can be truly enlightening. Our diary can also aid our discovery as to which soul-trait(s) we best need to work on at any one particular time.

Now let us look at chanting, visualisations and contemplations. These practices (like that of meditation – as described above) send messages and images directly to the deeper reaches of the soul – bypassing our intellect and ego. (Although I have written about these methods in my previous books, I am especially indebted to Alan Morinis for describing these suggestions in a clear and practical way).

CHANTING *(hitpa'alut):*

'The Hebrew term used for *Mussar* chanting means "with emotion," and, in fact, *Mussar* chanting is always emotional. Rabbi Salanter emphasised that the soul is directly influenced by the language of emotion, which it understands very well; and so he taught that chanting be done "with lips aflame." It also calls for a melody, as a phrase that is repeated in a singsong way. Rabbi Salanter recognised that melody is another modality that penetrates to the core of being where conscious thought can't reach.'

This concept is similar to 'meditation' as described above.

VISUALISATIONS:

'The practice of visualisations and contemplations follow similar logic. Holding vivid mental images in mind enlists the power of imagination to etch chosen messages directly to the soul. Strong mental impressions leave a trace that influences one's inner qualities, emotions, perceptions, judgment, and behaviours. The intellect is not the most profound of the aspects of soul - it is not the root; but impressions (wholesome and unwholesome) gathered in the mind do pass down to the root - and colour and shape the soul-traits.

This ability to visualise is so important to *Mussar* practice that when Rabbi Yechezkel Levenstein asks the question "What is the difference between a righteous person and a sinner?" he brings what he himself calls "a surprising answer" from the Alter of Kelm: "It is the ability to picture things in one's mind as if they were real."'

CONTEMPLATIONS:

'Contemplations are similar to visualisations; except in place of vivid images, the mind focuses on having an intense experience of a concept.'

Let the concept of you being the best person you can be truly excite you; focus strongly on this concept (Contemplation). Then actually *see* yourself giving help to another (Visualisation). What colour shirt/top are you wearing? Are you outside or inside? Do you feel cold or warm? Can you smell anything pleasant such as fresh flowers or fresh bread? Now say or sing out loud "I enjoy being the best I can be; when I'm doing good, I'm uniquely me." (Chanting/Affirmation).

How do we put these skills into daily practice? Alan Morinis suggests that we do a 'morning practice' chant followed by *kabbalot* (*mussar* work on the trait we are working on – to be done during the day) and lastly a *chesbon hanefesh* - literally an accounting of the soul; this is a review of the work that we have done during the day. Let's now see how it works in practice.

MORNING PRACTICE:

'Every morning, read over the phrase of the soul-trait of the week slowly and with full concentration. Read it aloud. Read it several times. Or chant (or sing) it to yourself. Go over this reminder in whatever way will cause it to be so clearly illuminated in your mind that it seems to be written in neon. Once you've really heard the phrase in so penetrating a way, go on with your day.'

DAYTIME PRACTICE:

Morinis gives some examples of *Kabbalot* (*Mussar* practices that we may choose to do during the day). For example, we may have chosen to work on the soul-trait of humility, gratitude or simplicity. Our actions *(kabbalot)* may then be:

Humility - Sit in the back of the room or hall

Gratitude - Give thanks to every inanimate thing that sustains you

Simplicity - Acquire nothing nonessential

BEDTIME/EVENING PRACTICE:

'At bedtime, pull out your notebook and try to identify events in your day that might reveal the presence of the specific quality you are working on for that week. Do this by recording (in your diary) all relevant incidents, thoughts and experiences that relate to that particular quality. This is a different use of the journal than when you were recording anything that revealed a soul-trait so you could compose your list of (specific) traits (that you needed to work on). Now you are using the evening writing practice to gain insight and clarity on the one trait that is your focus for the week.

THE JOURNAL IS NOT AN EVALUATION BUT RATHER A BRIEF, FACTUAL RECORD OF THE APPEARANCE OF THE DAILY TRAIT IN YOUR LIFE.'

One further thought

It is important to remember that we are here on Earth to make the physical holy. For example, we say blessings before and after food in order to make our act of eating into a holy one. Similarly, we (try to) adopt character traits that are attributed to G-d, so as to become more holy people.

The soul-traits in this book are all connected to G-d's wisdom. By working diligently to master and realise them, we can create our own joy, happiness and fulfilment.

Thus whenever we need to access any one of them, we will have that appropriate soul-trait at our fingertips. This should be the aim of all of us.

CHAPTER 1 – THE SOUL TRAIT OF FAITH

"My faith creates a life of meaning"

FAITH

What does it mean to have faith in G-d? And if we do have faith, how might it make a difference to our lives?

Let us first turn to Christophe Andre in his book *Mindfulness - 25 Ways to Live in the Moment Through Art.* He states:

'We must learn to live with uncertainty. Uncertainty is a source of anxiety. All forms of anxiety can be ultimately brought down to an intolerance of uncertainty. When we are tormented by thoughts of the future and death it's because these are our two greatest uncertainties. We try to limit uncertainty in our lives by insuring ourselves and taking precautions, or by endlessly checking and rechecking, running the risk that all these attempts at protection will wear us out and build barricades around our lives. We try to fill our minds with certainties, but without really reassuring ourselves. We know perfectly well, deep down, that all our efforts are pointless......For the truth is that there are insoluble problems in our lives and we have to accept them. We must accept them, but not contract around them. We must keep living and going forward, carrying their insolubility with us.

We must learn to live with doubt, with not knowing what to think or do.....Often we have no option but to say to ourselves, "I don't know, I can only doubt." But this doubt should not stop us choosing and acting when we must.'

Andre is basically saying that we should learn to live with our doubts about the future; yet still carry on making choices the best we can.

Yet, could G-d be an answer to our nagging uncertainties? We need to pose the question again: "What does having faith in G-d mean?" And if we do have faith, how might it make a difference to our lives?

My instinctive reaction to these questions is that having faith in G-d gives meaning to our life. Once we believe that a loving G-d exists, whatever happens (or will happen) in our lives has meaning. Everything is now not random; everything has meaning. G-d created us for a purpose.

But what about the bad things in life? The people that die before they have reached a ripe old age. Or the physical, emotional and yes spiritual pain that we will surely all experience at some time.

The Lubavitcher Rebbe wisely said:

"(When we ask) why is this not the way it is supposed to be? That itself is belief in G-d."

He is saying that when we ask why things turn out differently from what we expect (or from what we think we deserve) we are at least displaying our belief that G-d should be loving and caring - and thus *should* be giving us happiness, health and a long life.

Admittedly, if we make mistakes or go off the correct path, maybe we deserve a wake-up call – but surely not the scary shock of a shrill alarm clock. Rather a gentle reminder; a loving touch and encouragement from G-d that we should do and be better.

Well, that's my view anyway. I'll say it clear and loud. I think that G-d is too harsh sometimes. I think He should offer us more 'carrot' than 'stick'.

The truth is that perhaps my belief in a *loving* G-d is shaken when I see all the bad things that happen in this world; yet my faith in G-d, Himself, is not weakened.

Intellectually, I know that G-d's vision is all-encompassing - whereas mine is limited. Intellectually, I understand that G-d knows the right way to run the world. Emotionally, though, I don't always feel this.

Just as I sometimes think that I could run the English football team better than the current England manager can (actually he has just been sacked); or that I could do better than the British Prime Minister (actually he has just resigned....); sometimes I think I could run the world better than G-d. Except that I couldn't.

G-d created the world and gave me life. He expects great things of me. He tests me, He wants me to grow and break free from my comfort zone. I admit I don't understand everything - but I do have faith that G-d knows best.

By keeping *Shabbat* (the Jewish Sabbath), for example, we are demonstrating our faith that just as G-d created the world and then rested, so we should be able to cease our creative activities for one day a week. With faith that the world will keep on spinning round without our efforts.

"The body needs air. What is the air of the soul? Faith." says Rabbi Eliyahu Lopian in Lev Eliyahu.

Rabbi Dessler meanwhile posits that 'everything that occurs is a miracle and that there is no essential difference between the natural and the miraculous.'

How do we begin to bring such concepts into our awareness, though? The answer is by developing a sense of **awe** (see Chapter Nine).

Examining any aspect of the natural world (says Alan Morinis) ought to bring us to awesome awareness and appreciation. How can a hummingbird have such an iridescent throat? Who painted the butterfly's wings? How can the wonder that is a giraffe or a blue whale even be conceived (he asks)?

The miracle of life. The miracle of nature. Of the sun, moon and stars. Of human beings, animals and plant life. Did everything come to be through chance - or through a Divine Being?

And if we have faith that that Divine Being, G-d created all for a purpose, what effect does this have on us? It gives us the responsibility to investigate what our purpose in life is.

Yet we may still have uncertainty about the future, as Christophe Andre elucidated.

Rabbi Lopian attempts to allay these fears. He says:

"One whose faith in G-d is firm and perfect...automatically possesses ease of mind...."

That is because by having faith we begin to ask helpful questions such as:

"If this circumstance is happening for a purpose, how should I react to it purpose-fully? What meaning can I find from it? How can I turn (perceived) bad into good?"

Faith at least gives us the certainty that we are here for a reason; that we each have our unique life-mission. It also provides us with some excellent questions (such as those above) to which we need to find the answers.

We may still have some uncertainty – but our investigation has led to us moving forward. We can explore more; but we can also choose and act as Christophe Andre suggests. Faith is our beginning step on a wonderful, meaningful journey.

(For more on this fascinating topic, please see *Why Does G-d Let Bad Things Happen to Good People* on page 265)

FAITH (and Love)

If we have faith that G-d runs the world and does everything for a specific reason - even if we don't understand that reason - then we will not worry when things don't totally go our way.

If we have faith that G-d made us for a reason - with our own unique purpose - then we shall wish to find that purpose.

If we have faith that our skills, defects and flaws were given to us for a reason, then we will love and indulge in our abilities for the good of all.

Similarly we will love our flaws too. We will know that they are there - precisely so we can improve on them. We will laugh at them and enjoy their idiosyncratic nature!

The secret of both Judaism and *Mussar* (Jewish ethical learning) is balance.

For instance, I know that bad customer service frustrates me. Yet conversely - to balance this up - G-d has given me a talent for dealing with the bad service of others. This neatly corresponds with the Jewish precept that G-d only gives us challenges that we can cope with.

So I can argue well. I can win compensation. I can point out faults.

The wonderful thing is that G-d gave me the skills to deal with my challenges before he gave me the actual challenges themselves. Yet G-d also gave me a weakness for obsessing too much, for example, over what to put into complaints letters. Why?

G-d, in His infinite wisdom, wants me to use the skills and abilities He has given me - for the good - **without letting my negative emotions take over**. G-d wants me to work on myself; to master the soul-trait of faith.

If we have faith that it is G-d who is really causing us to experience whatever current problems we happen to have *(for our own good)* then we will learn to smile and shake off our concerns and worries. We will want to deal with our circumstances in a focused and good-natured way. This is one way of serving G-d.

If, in addition, we are able to love G-d like we would love a loving and caring father (for instance) then we will realise that He has our best interests at heart - even if we don't completely understand His reasoning.

If we learn to love others more, then we will see any behaviours of theirs that we don't like, simply as that (i.e. behaviours that we don't like). We may dislike some of their actions, but we will love the person nevertheless (except in extreme cases such as when a person is violent).

If we love ourselves more - and have faith in ourselves to deal with things with a pleasant disposition – then we will know that we can cope with our challenges without experiencing damaging emotions. Love is the emotion that will prevail.

Faith in ourselves that we can improve our *middot* (character/soul-traits) is the foundation of *Mindful Judaism*. Expressing love to ourselves and others will smooth this process considerably - and pave the way for a more enjoyable experience of life.

By the end of this book, it is my sincere wish that all of us will have learned to have loved a little more.

FAITH

Droplets of fine rain
Bring ongoing pain
Why is this all happening to me?

Stress never cares stop
When will G-d please drop
Actions with which I disagree?

What rhyme or reason
Snow out of season
Happiness running far away?

Wish I could believe
Black dog will soon leave
Depression transforming to play

Yet when faith appears
Sky magically clears
I understand what it's all for

Bad things fade and pass
G-d's simple life class
In valuing good things once more

Now I become well
Love touch, sight and smell
Abilities, skills and good friends

Know G-d wants of me
Best person to be
I pray that my life never ends
I pray only goodness, G-d sends.

NUMBER ONE – FAITH

'The eternal declaration of Jewish faith is *shema yisrael hashem elokanu hashem echod* - Hear O' Israel, Hashem is our G-d, Hashem is the One and Only. This is one of the first verses we are taught as children and the statement we make with our last dying breath: our moral testimony to G-d, the immortal source of all existence. Jewish life centres upon the awe-inspiring realisation that He is the Source of everything and existence revolves around Him.'

Jewish Wisdom in the Numbers

(Osher Chaim Levene and Rabbi Yehoshua Hartman)

In Judaism, the number 1 is inextricably associated with: G-d. There is 1 G-d in Jewish belief; no intermediaries as in Christianity. Jews believe that G-d created the world and that the *Torah* (Old Testament) is the word of G-d. Unlike, for example, in Christianity, Jews believe that nothing can be added to or subtracted from the *Torah*. Thus any so-called *New* Testament is, by definition, at odds with Jewish belief.

If we believe that a loving G-d created the world, it follows that there is a reason for this and thus our lives must have meaning and purpose. Even though we may not understand the workings of G-d's 'brain', we nonetheless understand that everything is not random; that what you and I do really matters.

We can, therefore choose to be a force for good - or otherwise. Yet, even if we go astray sometimes, we must continue to believe (and have faith).

G-d has given us numerous opportunities to re-start our lives and re-build our personalities; especially each *Rosh Hashana* (Jewish New Year), *Yom Kippur* (Day of Atonement) and each *Rosh Chodesh* (beginning of the Jewish month).

It is interesting that the Day of Atonement, the most holy day of the Jewish year, can be read as the day of **at one ment** - a further link between the number 1 and having faith in G-d.

THE INNER SECRET OF FAITH

Have you ever noticed that when people or systems don't behave the way you want them to, you sometimes become frustrated?

It could be because you've been kept waiting too long on the phone to speak to a receptionist.

Or that you've been irritated by a motorist who has driven too fast or too slow; or sworn at you when it is he or she who has driven badly.

All this is just the tip of the iceberg. A dear beloved late great aunt of mine apparently once said "hell is other people!" Sometimes I think I know what she was trying to say.

Yet the Jewish view is that everything is from G-d. That is if someone says or does something bad to you, he or she is just G-d's messenger giving you a wake-up call. This is not to say that G-d made that person commit a specific act; Judaism asserts that we have free-will.

The Jewish view is that G-d somehow uses a person's chosen action to have an impact on us. If it had not been that person causing us emotional stress, it would have been someone else doing something similar.

By having faith, we believe that everything is from G-d; thus our job is not to get too upset – but to focus on making the best response we can, instead.

Yet whilst on an intellectual level we may agree with this; emotionally it is often hard for us to believe that an all-powerful loving G-d wants anything even remotely bad to happen. Yes, there is the concept of reward and punishment that says we need to be 'punished' for our mistakes.   But G-d is meant to be merciful, so surely any 'punishment' should be small - such as the famous *Talmudic* example of putting our hand into our pocket and finding the wrong coin. That's punishment enough for me!

Yet if we had more faith, then we would believe that G-d always does everything for the best – even if, as mere human beings, we are not necessarily able to understand His reasoning.

As we indicated earlier on in the chapter, a major aid to having faith is through awe. If we meditate on nature, huge mountains and deep seas; or on a beautiful flower or the gurgling laugh of a small child, we become more aware of what an amazing world G-d has created.

Yes, we can and should argue with G-d (just as our forefather *Abraham* did – when he pleaded for the people of Sodom and Gomorrah to be saved). Yet we should focus more on working on our **reactions** to events as former Chief

Rabbi Lord Sacks advises. Let us start by cultivating awe, not only for G-d's greatness, but also for the greatness that He has given to each and every one of us.

With this in mind, I hope that we will develop sufficient faith in *ourselves* to achieve that marvellous potential He has gifted us. In addition, by working assiduously on all the soul-traits in this book – this will help us overcome any obstacles we may encounter along the way.

In our daily prayers, we proclaim that G-d returns life to us each morning because He has faith in us to become better people. It is indeed reassuring to know that G-d has faith in us, but the real practical inner secret of faith is to proclaim this out loud.

One of the most special gifts that G-d has granted us is the power of *speech*. (Kabbalah connects speech to the first Jewish month of the year, *Nissan* – see *Kosher Happiness* – and thus it links to our first soul-trait of Faith).

Inspiration, whether gained from a moment of awe or wonder – or from just a thought or an idea from nowhere – is marvellous. But have you ever noticed how it can suddenly disappear or dissipate? How do we regain that wonderful, but fleeting, insight or feeling of confidence that seemed to banish all our fears?

Speech is the special tool that can transform our wavering emotions into solid blocks of certainty. It is the inner secret of faith and a primary means to acquiring it.

In this book and in my three previous works, I have included poetry - and invited you, the reader, to recite those poems with gusto. In my last book *Modern Day Psalms,* I also quote Rabbi Zelig Pliskin and others extolling the virtues of **reciting** *tehillim* (the Psalms) - as opposed to just reading them silently to ourselves.

This is because our words have power. Whole books have been written on the value of affirmations; powerful sentences that we recite so as they can enter our very soul. In fact G-d created the world through speech. This is surely the reason why Judaism advocates saying our prayers out loud rather than silently reading them to ourselves.

At the beginning of each chapter, I have thus inserted a key phrase for you, dear reader, to recite. Pithy words to remind you of the essence of each individual soul-trait. Try reciting these phrases along with the poem, in each chapter, that is specifically related to the soul-trait you are working on. Add, if you like, any other encouraging and inspirational words from this book that speak to you. Or, for that matter, any helpful ideas that develop from within. Then, watch your faith in G-d and yourself increase.

We were all created for a unique purpose. Say now: "I am created for a unique purpose" out loud. Repeat it once more with energy, joy and gusto. Let's do it. Let's speak it out and watch our faith grow!

PSALM 118 – A PSALM INSPIRING FAITH

This is the day that Hashem (G-d) has made. We will rejoice and be happy in it

(Verse 24)

'Apply this verse to all three time zones; past present and future. First to the present: on this day when you are reading this. You are utilising this moment of this day, to reflect on how *Hashem* created this day. So rejoice. Let the joy spread from head to toe. Let this joy become an essential part of who you are.

Secondly, mentally visualise yourself having this joy in the days that you will experience from now on. On all days you can connect with *Hashem*. On all days you can elevate yourself spiritually.

And thirdly, you can look back at your past days. Rewrite those days with the knowledge and awareness that you presently have. See the hand of *Hashem* in your life. Gain an even greater appreciation for the happier days of your life. With your present lens, see how *Hashem* made each day to challenge you to become greater than the day before.'

Rabbi Zelig Pliskin *(Growth through Tehillim)*

Having faith creates a life of meaning. By reciting the above verse of Psalm 118 with gusto and belief, we can transform our past, present and future into days of joy and fulfilment.

Mindful visualisation for healing

Visualise Moses taking the Jewish people out of Egypt with steadfast faith; knowing how meaningful and vital it is to follow G-d's commandments. Imagine you can feel his joy and sense of confidence in carrying out this important *mitzvah* (commandment) of leading the Israelites to freedom.

Now, relax your body, drop your shoulders and breathe deeply. Close your eyes lightly and have a soft smile on your face as you visualise yourself having faith that everything that happens is for a reason – even if you don't yet understand that reason. Self-massage your face and neck – and feel reassured, secure and good in yourself.

CHAPTER 2 - THE SOUL TRAIT OF ORDER

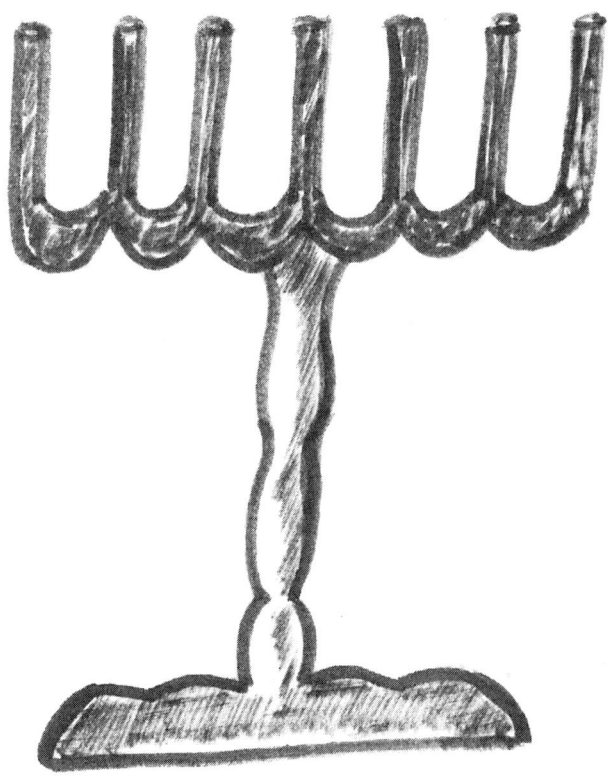

"A tidy ordered home leads to a settled mind"

ORDER

What is the relationship between our inner feelings and traits - and our outer surroundings and circumstances?

Let us, first of all, examine how our outer surroundings may affect us. On *Pesach* (the Jewish Passover) we scrupulously free our homes from *chametz* (bread and other prohibited foods for Passover); naturally doing a spring clean at the same time. At the end of this process our home is tidy and in order. We then engage in a Passover meal called a *Seder*. It is surely no coincidence that *seder* is the Hebrew word for order.

Our spick and span house, our well-ordered table, our special festival clothes; all these seem to create an inner alignment of safety and calm within ourselves.

Yet as Christophe Andre points out, sometimes in our lives our circumstances are not ideal and the going gets tough. At these times, we may not be able to seek refuge in the stimulus and structures of a Jewish festival or *Shabbat* (the Jewish Sabbath). It is then we need to motivate ourselves towards structured, goal-directed thinking to help us engage in positive action:

'Sometimes we feel so bad that we have to take refuge in action alone.....maintaining our efforts to survive without thinking. Because we know that thinking when we are unhappy can generate even more unhappiness and blindness. So we just actively do something. We need to have an overall sense of what's good or necessary for us, in other words to have thought a bit about it beforehand!'

(This advice fits in well with the soul-sense of the second month of the Jewish year, *Iyar;* whose soul sense is 'thought' - according to the oldest Kabbalistic book called the *Sefer Yetzirah).*

The point is that we may need to prepare **in advance** of any potential problems - with ordered and structured thinking – so that we are ready to cope with any challenges that may appear later on. This is why we emphasise, in this book, the practice of working on our soul-traits *before* we may actually need them. Thus when we face difficult times (outer conflicts), our inner soul-traits will be able to be accessed and to come into effect.

Christophe Andre goes on to explain how our inner preparation can lead us to take much-needed action. Even at a most basic level this can prove vital:

'(With such preparation) we can carry out some action, in total humility. We do this because we know that it will help us survive. We go for a walk, do the garden, tidy up, make something or work. We don't do this in order to escape or feel better but because there's nothing else we can do and if we do nothing we'll go under. It's not fun, it doesn't make us feel good, but sometimes life is like that.'

Tidying up our homes and having structure in our lives is vitally important as Frumma Rosenberg-Gottlieb explains:

'Attention to the small details is also a characteristic of mindfulness. A calm soul is reflected in a balanced and orderly outer environment. Thinking peacefully and being in the moment help us pay greater attention to the small things—and vice versa. Keep your home, your car, and your office uncluttered; become more proficient at saying no to requests that aren't in line with your priorities. Staying organised and balanced will help you keep from overtaxing yourself, and can help reduce the level of stress you experience in your life. *Torah* literature describes a well-ordered environment as a balm to the soul.'

Alan Morinis adds: 'Keeping a tidy home and a well-ordered life honours those you relate with.' He continues:

'The soul-traits of honour and **humility** (see Chapter Six) help us maintain this outer order because:

Being humane stops us rebelling against order. Instead of saying the words "I don't want (to tidy up or to look presentable)", having humility makes us think of the effect it will have on the other rather than ourselves.'

From the above we can see that whereas our inner traits can help us maintain order in our lives – having order and structure can similarly affect how we feel inside.

Shabbat (The Jewish Sabbath) particularly helps brings order to our lives - as do the Jewish festivals. However unstructured his life is, the believing and observant Jew somehow manages to get himself and his/her home in order, ready for *Shabbat* and the Jewish festivals.

The month of *Iyar* (see above) is without any major festivals. However, it is notable as being the only full month in the Jewish year when we count the *Omer*. I quote from chabad.org:

'The Kabbalists explain that the 49 days that connect Passover with Shavuot correspond to the 49 drives and traits of the human heart. Each day saw the refinement of one of these *sefirot*, bringing the people of Israel one step closer to their election as G-d's chosen people and their receiving of His communication to humanity.

Each year, we retrace this inner journey with our "Counting of the Omer." Beginning on the second night of Passover, we count the days and weeks: "Today is one day of the Omer"; "Today is two days of the Omer"; "Today is seven days, which are one week of the Omer"; and so on, till "Today is forty-nine days, which are seven weeks of the Omer." Shavuot, the "Festival of Weeks," is the product of this count, driven by the miracles and revelations of the Exodus but achieved by a methodical, 49-step process of self-refinement within the human soul.'

So during this period of *the Counting of the Omer*, we are given the opportunity to work on our character traits in an ordered and structured way.

Our sense of order can also be increased by looking at harmonious art, listening to peaceful music and walking in beautifully well-ordered parks or gardens.

It is, in addition, helpful to set fixed times for learning and everything else in our lives. Having a disciplined structure is all important – even more so if we regard ourselves as generally unstructured.

We may love the creative flow of instinctive poetry; or crave for inspiration and spontaneity. We may adore the type of humour that turns round our bored perspective of life.

Yet like the improvisational pianist, we need to first of all master the simple chords and scales. Paradoxically, we need structure and order - *before* we can experiment and break free from their constrictions.

I remember a singer-songwriter of the 1970's, Christopher Rainbow, once saying that whilst he likes to take his audience out on a journey of discovery - he always returns them to the safety of (a structured, metaphorical) home.

I rephrase his words, but his concept is clear. We can and must explore and investigate. We must get off the well-worn beaten track sometimes; it is healthy and invigorating to do so. As long as we know we can (when we need to) return to our metaphorical (or actual) home - to a place of safe order.

Judaism accentuates balance. Ecclesiastes suggests that there is 'a time to weep and a time to laugh, a time to mourn and a time to dance.....' Inner order is termed **equanimity** (see Chapter Four). Order and structure are the key to creative achievement. They are akin to the safety net that enables the tightrope walker to boldly go forward without fear.

Another concept of 'order' is to take things **in order**, one by one. Yissachar is the tribe connected to the second month of the Jewish year, *Iyar,* which corresponds to our second soul-trait of order. His was the tribe that was responsible for time-planning – see *Kosher Happiness* for more.

It is very easy to worry about something that may or not happen in a few days or a month's time. Being mindful is about dealing with 'first things first' with everything at its rightful time. This is a much less stressful way of approaching our lives; a philosophy well worth living by.

ORDER (and Love)

How does cultivating the soul-trait of order help us to love ourselves more?

Being orderly, structured and tidy is actually of great assistance. Dressing smartly on the *Shabbat* (Jewish Sabbath) - or at any other time for that matter – makes us look and feel better. We are respecting ourselves - and other people notice that. Thus they begin to respect us too. Contrast dressing in an unkempt and untidy way. If we do so, hopefully our friends and family will still love us. But others? What if we don't bother to wash or take care of ourselves? How will others react to us then?

An orderly home similarly makes us feel better. By taking more control of our space - we feel more in control of our lives, too.

The festival of *Pesach* (Passover) is *the* festival of order. On the first two nights (just the first in Israel) we enjoy a Passover meal called a *Seder*. And, as we have previously noted, the Hebrew word *seder* means 'order'.

On the second night of this eight day festival, we begin to count the *Omer*. Kabbalah tells us that the first week of the *Omer* corresponds to the trait of *chesed* (loving-kindness). Our order *(seder)* thus begins an act of love!

When we look at an 'orderly' (structured and harmonious) painting or listen to an ordered (melodious) piece of music, it helps balance our emotions. Similarly when there is order in society, we seem more peaceful within ourselves.

Feeling good leads to calm and helps us to love ourselves and others more. The order created by knowing that there is a *Shabbat* every week for us to rest and enjoy - can be both exhilarating and a relief! In general, the Sabbath day seems to bring out the best in people. It is not surprising, therefore, that love and regard for others is more likely to be experienced on this day than during the rest of the week.

The same applies with regard to the Jewish festivals. These stand like oases in time - periods when we can stop and take stock of ourselves. Ideally, on these blessed and holy days, we dress smartly and our homes are tidy and in order.

Such conditions allow love to flow more easily.

ORDER

Yissachar became the master of time;

I feel out of sorts when my life doesn't rhyme
If you want for someone who keeps you await
I'm the prime guy you should choose for a date!

Must truly admit, though, I can't organise
Genius has its downside, please sympathise
Like juggler whose balls seem to float in the air
Structure makes me want to pull out my hair

How envy I, those, with regular lives
Steady jobs - certainty - immaculate wives
And me, I'm still searching for life *ordinaire*
Knowledge how to act - loving wife to care

Yet there are those moments too precious to miss
Inspiring...creative...leading to pure bliss

Zevulun, it was he, who earned all the money;

That'll never be me, though, don't laugh, it's not funny

If only I'd brought order to my soul
I'd be famous actor - in chief starring role
If structure and free-flow were able to fuse
My floatiness - I'd be able to lose

A calm stable life would be what I'd choose

With this poem, hope, I've been able to schmooze!

NUMBER TWO – ORDER

The number 2 is, on the face of it, a number of division and conflict. As *Jewish Wisdom in the Numbers* explains:

'The first example of such division was Day 2 of the Creation when G-d divided the waters in the formation of the Heavens above and the oceans below. The phrase "it was good," used to describe G-d's assessment of the other days of creation, is glaringly absent on Day 2, when conflict and division first appeared.'

Yet 2 can also be a number of perfect symmetry and order. Again from *Jewish Wisdom in the Numbers:*

'The spectacular symmetries within the natural world can be seen in plant leaves, the wings of a butterfly, the structure of crystals, and the formation of snowflakes. Perhaps the most intricate projection of symmetry is the anatomical design of the human being. The numerous pairs of limbs and organs in the body include the eyes, eyebrows, nostrils, ears, cheeks, lips, shoulders, arms, hands, legs, ankles, and feet. Here the corresponding pairs within Creation need not be considered contradictory; the opposites become the amazing reflection of the other.'

The number 2 also brings to mind another pair - a man and wife. When any 2 people have their lives in order, they will have a much better chance of forming a relationship than 2 people who don't.

Physical order can affect spiritual order. This means that when our physical surroundings, such as our living spaces and the way we dress are orderly, we find it easier to focus on our spirituality.

Similarly spiritual order (Jewish observance and character-trait development) can enhance our physical lives. Thus, when we feel spiritual, we are more likely to love our neighbour and have harmony in our relationships.

In summary, it is fair to say that the number 2 both needs and has the potential for order.

When order is manifest both within and without, there is more likelihood of us experiencing inner peace. In organisations and countries, conflict will fade and harmony will be the new normal.

THE INNER SECRET OF ORDER

I am always in a rush.

I am that sort of person who expects roads to be empty, traffic lights always green and pedestrians to happily stop and wave me on my way - so I can get to my destination on time (or perhaps only five minutes late).

Except, things never quite seem to work out that way - and, as usual, I'm madly rushing, rushing, rushing and still being late!

So, the soul-trait I need is order. I need to plan my time more carefully - and I thought I did exactly that today. I awoke half an hour earlier; yet I still ended up leaving home ten minutes later that I would have wished.

However, I wasn't that late taking my washing to the launderette. The real delay came in the supermarket. It was a Sunday in London just six weeks before Xmas - and it was packed. Worse still was the queue for the free cup of coffee that the supermarket offers. They have two coffee machines, but today one wasn't working.....

So I was late, which meant I had to rush my lunch a little in order to get to the library computer – in time to type out these very words. Yet with better time-planning, it could all have been so much more pleasant and relaxed.

What more could I have done to allow myself more time? What is the inner secret that makes 'order' work for us?

The first answer to this conundrum lies in displaying a modicum of wisdom. Had I been wiser, I may well have approached things in a different way. For example, I might have left my washing till later in the day. This rearranging of my schedule would have saved a little time. Also, did I really have to go to the supermarket *today?* And even once I'd decided to go, couldn't I have avoided the queue at the busy coffee machine - by missing out on my beloved fix of caffeine for once in a blue moon?

So acquiring wisdom is a good answer, but it is not an easy quality to develop. To conjure up a more effective response, I have related my question to the specific system I have developed for this 'inner secret' section of the book.

What I have done is to connect each soul-trait to a Jewish month of the year; and to the particular soul-sense of that month (as detailed and explained in my book *Kosher Happiness)*. 'Order' is our second soul-trait and is thus related to the second month of the Jewish year *Iyar* whose special sense (decreed by Kabbalah) is **thinking**.

I had planned my morning in a specific order; this was the right thing to do and it resulted in me doing most of the things I wanted to do in fairly good (if a little rushed) time. What I failed to do, however, was to adapt when I saw time running away from me. I needed to take a moment to think and to re-prioritise.

Would it have been so bad to have done my washing later on? Would it have been so disastrous if I had gone to the supermarket on another day? Would it have been so terrible to have missed out on my free cup of coffee? A few moments of careful thought could have saved me valuable time, led to a more relaxed lunch - and perhaps have put me in a great mood, too!

Iyar is the second month of the Jewish year; its special sense is correct thinking. It is no surprise then that 'thought' is the inner secret of order.

PSALM 90 – A PSALM INSPIRING ORDER

You reduce humans to pulp. And you say "repent"

(Verse 3)

In this chapter, we have focused on the importance of having order and structure in our lives. The above verse from Psalms (according to Rabbi Zelig Pliskin) helps remind us of this. He explains:

'We human beings always need reminders. We tend to get used to a situation that has remained constant for some time. People who are responsible and organised use various methods to remember to take care of what they must do.

Yom Kippur (The Day of Atonement) is a day that is totally dedicated to Teshuvah (repentance and return to G-d).

Throughout the prayers on this holy day, we repeat that we deeply regret the wrongs that we have done. Fine, but what about the rest of the year? How do we remember then, that we need to improve?

Adversity and suffering serve as reminders during the rest of the year, and it is very important that we keep in mind that this is the purpose of those reminders. (For example) aches and pains might be a minor message or they might be a sign that something is seriously wrong. From the above verse in Psalm 90, we see that all suffering is a spiritual reminder. Hashem (G-d) is telling us, "I care about you and your eternal soul. Wake up! Pay attention! Make the necessary corrections."'

The above verse from Psalms thus reminds us that even pain and suffering can be used for the good, if we adopt an orderly and structured response to them.

Mindful visualisation for healing

Visualise a beautifully well-ordered seder table, full of Jewish symbolism; especially prepared for the Jewish festival of Pesach (Passover).

Three matzas (unleavened bread) wrapped in a white cloth. Bottles of red, kosher for Pesach wine. Plates, cutlery and wine glasses neatly set out for each guest. The seder plate is immaculately arranged with shank-bone, hard-boiled egg, bitter herbs, vegetable (parsley or lettuce) and charoset (a delicious mixture of apples, nuts and wine).

Let this structured festive scene remind you of the importance of having order in your life – as you say to yourself:

"A tidy and ordered home leads to a settled mind."

CHAPTER 3 - THE SOUL TRAIT OF ENTHUSIASM

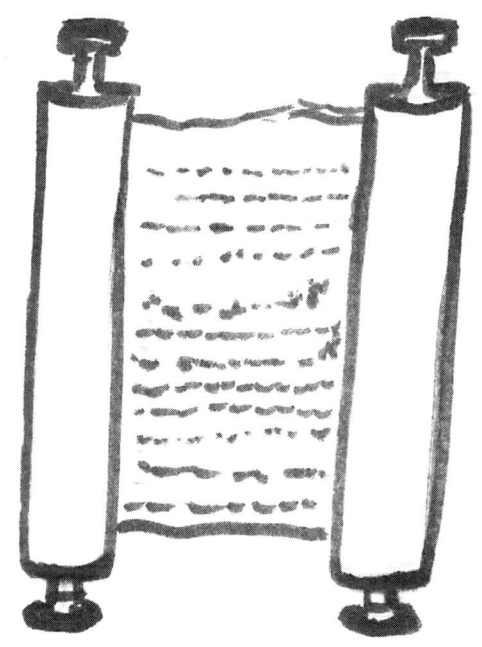

"Enthusiasm – The fuel that propels us to greatness"

ENTHUSIASM

We instinctively know that enthusiasm is a wonderful soul-trait to have.

We can see this from the words of Alan Morinis:

'If you are going to be generous, how much better to give with enthusiasm.'

In the same vein he advises: 'Be *zealous* in defence of the honour of your friend.'

Yet how can we achieve this wonderful trait of zeal and enthusiasm? Rabbi Moshe Chaim Luzzatto (the *Ramchal)* has a suggestion:

"Just as enthusiasm can *result* from an inner burning, so it can *create* one. That is, one who perceives a quickening of his outer movements in the performance of a *mitzvah* (commandment) conditions himself to experience a flaming inner movement, through which his longing and desire will continually grow."

He is basically saying that outer movement inspires and encourages inner movement - just as an inner burning or desire can create enthusiasm. So perhaps, in our quest for enthusiasm, we should exercise, dance, walk, stretch, smile....or even act out our inner desire of how we wish to be.

The Ramchal also counsels that recognising our role in life will counter worry - and that when we have firm **trust** (see Chapter Eight) that whatever will be, will be as G-d wants it to be, there will simply be no place in our heart for baseless anxiety.

Alan Morinis affirms that worrying and fretting can deplete our spiritual energy. In fact (he says) anxiety is what often underlies things we do that sap our enthusiasm. Thus we can see the benefits of developing trust are great.

Following our heart with enthusiasm is a wonderful recommendation, too. This prevents too much focus on rationalisation - another zeal-sapper!

Acting spontaneously is another way in which we can counteract excessive deliberation and laziness - two other things that conspire to weaken our enthusiasm.

So we need trust, spontaneity and, I would argue, exciting goals in life to motivate us.

Cultivating **awe** (see Chapter Nine) will surely enthuse and excite us, too. By looking up at the magnificent skies, for instance, we will soon become aware of G-d's marvellous creation – which we are a part of! This will lead us to realise that we have great potential - as we have a spark of Godliness within us.

Recognising that we therefore have the ability to develop thrilling life goals will lead us to become enthused - propelling us to achieve many great things.

I passionately believe that meditating on music, art and colours we like - along with reading inspiring ideas and stories - can really get us moving too.

ENTHUSIASM (and Love)

When we are enthusiastic about something or someone, we are less likely to be so self-absorbed - or focused on general day-to-day worries. Instead, we feel good, excited and animated; we love ourselves and others more. Music, sports or a new love may have this effect on us. So might exciting or creative ideas or Jewish spiritual concepts.

'Do what you love and find ways of loving what you do.'

I am excited by the fact that I may have just invented the above saying - even though I am pretty sure that someone, somewhere, must have thought of it first.

Yet, in the hectic times we live in, it is so easy to focus on negative things or to play the same worry tape over and over again in our mind. Far better to STOP and remind ourselves of people, ideas, books, paintings or plays that we love instead.

Shouldn't we feel guilty, though, about focusing on the pleasures of life - rather than being involved in something more serious? Not necessarily. Rabbi Nachman tells us, in fact, that 'it's a mitzvah to be happy' whilst Judaism advises that depression is bad for us and can lead to sin.

The truth is that we must have balance in our lives. For example, we may sometimes get excited over Judaism's *concepts;* whilst at other times, we may choose to engage in intellectual pursuit of its *wisdom.*

In fact, we are, specifically encouraged to study Jewish texts and ideas that we enjoy. What's more, whether our love is science, the arts or psychology - we will find related Jewish texts to inspire and enthuse us.

Science - How about investigating the creation of the world through studying the *torah* (biblical) portion of Genesis along with some kabbalistic (Jewish mystical) concepts that discuss this.

Drama, film and art – Why not look at Judaism through the lens of the arts. The story of Esther is sheer theatre. The crossing of the Reed Sea is pure cinema. The talking ass in the *torah* portion of Balak is almost fantasy. Paint a picture or act out any of these wondrous scenes.

Psychology - How and why do people act the way they do? How do we become the best person we can be? A wealth of Jewish books (like those of Rabbi Zelig Pliskin for example) will provide enough psychological stimulation for the most enquiring of minds.

Very soon, we will start to love our Judaism; love G-d for giving us the ability to be enthusiastic and love ourselves for being creative. Won't we then love others too?

ENTHUSIASM

Let's invent something sparkling new
Pray fervently like a good Jew
Smile at everyone we know
They'll smile back; our love will flow

Today my life began again
Journeyed to you on the Blue Train
There's nothing that we cannot do
Enthusiasm's bloomed anew

Started a class in new ideas
Taught how to banish ancient fears
Ran marathon, walked half a mile
Painted her portrait with a smile

Enthusiasm - love the word!
Makes rigours of life seem absurd
Garden of Eden is more apt
Become G-d's gift that Eve unwrapped

Hit the road Jack, June, Jill and John
Moments to contemplate upon
We're going forward all the time
Realising life is so sublime

Enthusiasm - feels so good!
Join my journey, wish you would
Be on my team then you'll soon find
Enthusiasm's always kind

Follow the passion of your choice
Sing your own song in fullest voice
The secret of life's plain to see
Enthusiasm's you and me

Enthusiasm sets you free!

NUMBER THREE – ENTHUSIASM

What could the connection be between the number 3 and enthusiasm? *Jewish Wisdom in the Numbers* offers a clue. It tells us that:

'Every process can be divided into 3 stages. There is the beginning point, which articulates the objective at the very outset. This clearly defines the direction in which one is heading. Next there is the middle or interim phase, when man sets out into motion using all the tools at his disposal to actively pursue his goal. Lastly, there is the final phase, when man reaches his destination. Here he celebrates having attained his goal by arriving at the end.'

The above gives us a hint that the number 3 may be connected with celebration. A man and a woman adding a third (a baby) to their family also brings to mind the same idea. It is a wonderful event well worth celebrating.

Jewish Wisdom in the Numbers reminds us of another 3:

'The celebrations of the 3 (pilgrimage) festivals *(Pesach Shavuos* and *Succos)* are not simply commemorations of historic events that occurred on the same calendar dates; through them, the Jewish people actually relive the illumination of these past events, to undergo the same elevated spiritual experience. Thus, on *Pesach* they relive the spiritual freedom of the Exodus; on *Shavuos* they reaccept the *Torah:* and on *Succos* they live in booths under the protection of G-d.'

They are, thus 3 holy times of celebration. We celebrate these *chagim* (festivals) with delicious festive meals. When we celebrate, we do so naturally with enthusiasm. Our physical celebrations awaken our Jewish soul.

Lastly, *Jewish Wisdom in the Numbers* reminds us how the number 3 is connected to Jewish law and teachings - our holy *Torah:*

'The *Talmud* (commentary on the *Torah*) records that "G-d gave the 3-fold *Torah* to a 3-fold people through the 3rd-born child on the 3rd day in the 3rd Jewish month. The 3-fold *Torah* refers to the Written *Torah* that comprises the Five Books of the *Torah,* the Prophets and the Writings. The 3-Fold people are the nation of Israel that consists of 3 categories - *Kohen* (Priest); *Levi* (Levite); and *Yisrael* (ordinary Jew). The *Torah* was transmitted via Moshe, the 3rd of his parents' children. It was given at Sinai after 3 days of sanctification, in *Sivan,* the 3rd month of the Jewish calendar. *Krias HaTorah,* public *Torah* reading, was arranged to ensure that 3 days do not elapse without the congregation hearing the holy words of *Torah.* A minimum of 3 people must be called up to the *Torah* reading and each passage read must contain at least 3 verses.'

We are commanded to serve G-d with joy (Psalm 100: Verse Two). Our prayers and study of the *Torah* are part of this 'service to G-d.' The *Torah* is the life-blood of the Jewish people. Thus, if we are enthusiastic about our *Torah* study we will surely be serving *Hashem* (G-d) joyfully.

THE INNER SECRET OF ENTHUSIASM

Colin's personal *bete-noire* - the thing he hated most about himself - was his inability to approach someone he really wanted to talk to. Yesterday, it happened yet again. This time it was a pretty young woman - and yes, he had a good excuse for failing. She was sitting next to someone (whom he took to be her boyfriend) at a lecture - and at its conclusion she began to chat to this person. Although Colin had a split-second chance to talk to her before she left, he didn't quite manage to seize the opportunity.

What could Colin have done differently, with regard to the soul-traits in this book? 'Enthusiasm' is the trait that comes to mind. Had Colin worked on having enthusiasm at his disposal whenever he needed it, he may have succeeded in chatting to the young woman in question. Yet, by itself, would enthusiasm have been quite enough?

Especially when she was talking to the other guy; would Colin have summoned up enough courage to talk to her? Probably not. He would have needed something more than just plain enthusiasm. Courage certainly would have helped, but it is a hard trait to master. What Colin needed was something easier to acquire - the inner secret of enthusiasm…..

The third month of the Jewish year (that corresponds to our third soul-trait of enthusiasm) is the month of *Sivan* whose special sense is correct walking. The Hebrew word for this is *halicha* which is related to the word *halacha* (the body of the Jewish Law).

We can see a connection here as the month of *Sivan* marks the festival of *Shavuos* which is when the *Torah* (Jewish law and teachings) was given to the Jewish people.

To study the *Torah,* we need enthusiasm - but also (and even more so) inquisitiveness about its meanings and teachings. The inner secret of enthusiasm is thus *inquisitiveness.*

Inquisitiveness is what we have when we are a traveller (rather than a tourist); it is walking or journeying in an adventurous manner - driven by our desire to know more and explore.

If only Colin had been passionately inquisitive as to why the young lady was at the lecture - or whereabouts she lived, for example; the flame of enthusiasm would have burnt within him - and he would have instinctively found a way to approach her.

Had Colin really been inquisitive enough to find out about the young woman, he would have spoken to her in a natural manner. Enthusiasm may propel us to act, but it is by walking the way of inquisitiveness that will bring us onto the royal road of achieving this positive and desirable soul-trait.

PSALM 29 – A PSALM INSPIRING ENTHUSIASM

Hashem will bless His people with peace

(Verse 11)

'"The blessing of the Almighty is peace." The question to ask ourselves is, "What can I do personally for the sake of peace?" The first step to creating peace is in the way we talk to others. The contents of what we say and the tone of voice in which we say it, will be key factors in whether a disagreement or displeasure is expressed with mutual respect or the lack thereof.

"The value of the good we do is increased, when it is difficult." How can we prepare for a difficulty? Make a clear picture in your mind about how you can speak and act, in ways that are conducive to peace. Visualise yourself being respectful and dignified in the face of challenges. Just as professional actors practice their lines over and over again, we too might (do so).'

Rabbi Zelig Pliskin

We have described the values of enthusiasm throughout this chapter. Like 'peace', it is a vital soul-trait to acquire. We could, therefore replace the word 'peace' in the verse from Psalms above with the word 'enthusiasm.' Try it!

Enthusiasm, like peace, is a desirable quality that can propel us to greatness.

Mindful visualisation for healing

When the Jewish people went to receive the *Torah* (Jewish law and teachings) at Mount Sinai, in the third month of *Sivan*, it is said that they overslept. In an effort to atone for that moment, the Kabbalists of Safed instituted a special night of *Torah* study. This takes place on the first night of *Shavuos* – the festival that commemorates and relives the giving of the *Torah*.

Throughout that night, I personally attend *shiurim* (classes) – which are punctuated by plentiful amounts of welcome refreshment. It is both an illuminating and enjoyable occasion that I enthusiastically participate in.

Visualise yourself excitedly awaiting G-d's giving of the holy *Torah* – the guidebook to Jewish life. It is to be a powerful and awe-inspiring ceremonial moment at Mount Sinai - equal to a thousand Olympic opening and closing ceremonies. Now (after the event) see yourself speaking enthusiastically to others about your amazing experience and allow that special energy of encountering G-d's presence to permeate every part of your being.

CHAPTER 4 - THE SOUL TRAIT OF EQUANIMITY

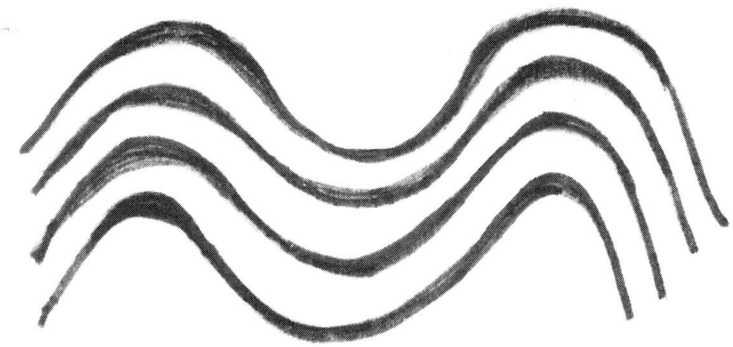

"With equanimity I gracefully accept life's ups and downs"

EQUANIMITY

When Rabbi Yisrael Salanter says that "as long as one lives a life of calmness and tranquillity in the service of G-d...he is remote from true service" - it shakes up our understanding of what life is all about.

Don't we truly want to be calm and tranquil most of the time? Yes, maybe we like to get excited over sports or music and life in general, but we certainly don't wish to get stressed out and anxious, do we?

Yet, it is notable that our most heartfelt and personal prayers to G-d come when we are feeling worried and dissatisfied. So perhaps Rabbi Salanter has a point.

Except that, rather than talking about prayer, he uses the expression *service of G-d*. If we want to 'serve' G-d properly, by doing good things *(mitzvot)*, surely we need to be calm and tranquil.

If we are angry, for instance, service to G-d is going to be difficult to say the least. Let us explore deeper by trying to understand the exact meaning of this soul-trait of equanimity – which can loosely be described as 'peace of mind.'

In *Uncovering Happiness,* Dr Elisha Goldstein states:

'Equanimity, the perfect partner to **compassion** (see Chapter Seven), brings stability, spaciousness, and balance to our hearts and minds. It's the ability to remain deeply present and open to what is here. It's allowing ourselves to know our pain or the pain of another without getting lost in it or overwhelmed by it.'

Alan Morinis refers to equanimity as 'calmness of the soul'. Yet he veers towards Dr Goldstein's view by also defining it as 'accepting turbulence and even turmoil - like a surfer riding the waves on an even keel - centred in oneself, yet sensitive to the forces (unexpected waves) all around.'

So it seems to be the *soul*, our most innermost point, that stays calm amongst the turbulence within and without of us - when we embrace equanimity.

The Jewish view, in fact, is that we are meant to have tests in life - in order to have opportunities to grow and draw closer to other people and G-d.

Our purpose is to rise above (Rabbi Leffin) - or better still distance ourselves (Rabbi Moshe ben Nachman and the Rosh) - from such traits as pride, anger and jealousy. Overcoming such feelings are examples of our 'personality tests'.

This is surely what Rabbi Salanter means when he says that "as long as one lives a life of calmness and tranquillity in the service of G-d...he is remote from true service." Our *service of G-d* is for us to become better people; to face the inevitable challenges that will surface by working to improve ourselves.

Observing the Jewish commandments *(mitzvot)* is one of the pathways we can take.

Working on our soul-traits is another; and as this book seeks to demonstrate, there are several ways to succeed in this.

Alan Morinis, for example, advises that 'meditation provides an inner witness.' He asserts that 'while sitting still and silent, many inner states will arise. (Yet, when this happens, we can practise) living in their presence without feeling that we are a slave to any of them.'

Another ruse includes FOCUSING *(*a soul-sense connected to the fourth Jewish month of *Tammuz* that corresponds to this fourth soul-trait of equanimity); on our ultimate life goals, or on nature for instance.

Walking (and observing) in a garden or park or by the sea is especially therapeutic. In addition, looking at a beautiful painting or immersing ourselves in a descriptive poem or moving piece of music are wonderful ways in which we can use the arts to calm the soul.

In addition, Alan Morinis on *jewishpathways.com* talks about the benefits gained when we can see and focus upon the 'inner light' in everyone and everything:

'Rabbi Steinsaltz describes the Jewish spiritual experience as a constant beckoning toward the light. If we take that word "constant" seriously, then the light we seek must be present at all times and in all situations, no matter how murky or even dark they appear to us. We are assured that it is there, and that we are capable of seeing it, but it is up to us to cultivate the inner sensors that are alert and attentive to it.

This can't be described any better than "inner light." The more we try to describe it, the less accurate is the description. Even calling it "light" is a metaphor. It is a presence that defies classification in the terms of this world, but is perceptible nonetheless.

Your practice for this period is to tune into the inner light that is present in all things and beings. This may not be easy to do at first, because we are not looking for *physical* light, but something more subtle. To start with, it is valuable just to pick out an object that is right near to hand and to ask the question, "Can I see the inner?" Look for a subtle, brilliant presence behind the apparent surface. In time, as you explore, you will begin to see what Rabbi Steinsaltz is pointing to. As you strengthen this practice, over time you will grow increasingly aware of the radiant Presence that is a constant in the ever-shifting contexts in which you live.

You can remind yourself several times a day to seek the inner light. If you have eyes to see, and if you are patient, it is there in all the people you meet, and in the telephone and the apple, too. Are you in a café? Take a different look at the coffee cup. Or are you in a classroom? Look at the blackboard, then look again. Can you glimpse the light within everything you see?

Record your experiences in your Accounting of the Soul Diary.

This is not a mystical practice, but mental training. By assigning your mind the task of looking for something that is to be found in every situation, you will cultivate and strengthen your inner witness. The outcome is that you will have equipped your mind with the capacity to anchor itself in a solid and tranquil place. From there you can observe life even amid the churning seas of emotion that arise in stormy episodes. Without this training, you are likely to be tossed about on the waves of inner feeling that wash through you; with it, you are capable of mooring your consciousness in the role of witness, and so be tranquil.

An inner eye connected to the constant light won't give you a life of fewer challenges and struggles. But it will help you develop the trait of equanimity, which will in turn helps you to engage and triumph. That's may be why the Alter of Kelm tells us: "A person who has mastered peace of mind, has gained everything."

Here are some suggested key-phrases for you to use:

"Rise above the good and the bad."
"Be still and witness." '

Christophe Andre prefers to define our challenge (regarding acquiring equanimity) and its resolution this way:

'When we are suffering very badly, when we are very unhappy, we cut ourselves off from the world. We no longer find it interesting. It seems indifferent, almost offensive to us. Yet, in its own way, it can help or save us. The more we suffer the more we must make sure we remain in contact with everything around us. Suffering is always increased and prolonged by separation and distance, by withdrawal into ourselves. I must train myself so that when I feel unhappy I still remain sensitive to the beauty of the world. Even if it doesn't ease my pain, even if it doesn't help me straight away. There will come a time when everything will shift and it will save me......

Take this passage from a book by (Jewish) Austrian psychiatrist Viktor Frankl, who survived Dachau concentration camp: "One evening, when we were already resting on the floor of our hut, dead tired, soup bowls in hand, a fellow prisoner rushed in and asked us to run out to the assembly grounds and see the wonderful sunset." This kind of behaviour is not escapism or a psychological defence mechanism to escape horror; it is an act of awareness and supreme intelligence. At a time when they are surrounded by an ocean of death, these human beings turn their minds to what is also beautiful in the world. They are powerless, lost and confused, but they do not abandon their humanity......

I remember an excellent study showing that people in mourning for a dead partner - who were able to smile as they talked about the person they had lost ('It's so painful to have lost him, but I'm so happy to have known him') - were also those who felt the best two years later, because they had the ability not to allow happiness to be overwhelmed by sadness.

They were able to understand that life consists of everything together, and that unhappiness does not invalidate past happiness or take it away from us. The happiness we have experienced remains ours forever. We are perfectly entitled to weep and smile at the same time - we do so because we accept the world (G-d's world, I would say, - Marvin J Shaw) and love it with all our might (by focusing on its goodness, I would add - Marvin J Shaw).'

Looking beyond the present moment and imagining more positive feelings that lie ahead can help restore our balance (Morinis). Or, we can achieve this by focusing on happy events from the past (as the previous example shows). Or by finding beauty and goodness in the present - as the Viktor Frankl story demonstrates. We just have to tease out the inner light in any situation. Alternatively, in times of distress, we may choose to pray or say a psalm instead.

Furthermore, even if we are in physical or emotional pain (G-d forbid) - by doing the right thing or purposefully living our life-mission, we can still feel an inner satisfaction, contentment and even joy (Rabbi Akiva Tatz).

Rabbi Shlomo Wolbe writes that the goal of all personal spiritual practice is to be at peace with one-self, with one's environment and with G-d. Rabbi Eliyahu Dessler explains how to reach that goal. He says it is impossible to concentrate when outside interests and desires cloud the mind. A settled mind is achieved primarily by *clearing the mind* of all else but the task at hand. He adds that when a person makes a little effort in this direction, he or she is awarded with Divine assistance, and that through the process of trying to achieve mental settled-ness, one comes to acquire *menuchat ha'nefesh* (tranquillity, a settled soul).

Alan Morinis says that the distractions of the mind are usually rooted in the specific *middot* (traits) that are in play for that person at that particular time and that these are the (specific) soul-traits in which that person has the potential to grow. He gives a personal example in telling us that planning is what tends to disturb his peace of mind. This indicates (he says) that he has a weakness in the trait of *bitachon* (**trust** - see Chapter Eight).

In truth, all of us need to equip ourselves with all twelve of the soul-traits. However, at any one time, some traits are stronger or weaker than others. By practising all twelve soul-traits on a regular basis, we shall be able to bring to the fore any particular one of them when we need it most.

We should thus expect many challenges in this life in our service of G-d. Yet by being prepared and cultivating equanimity (calmness of the soul) we shall prevail and overcome with a smile on our face and peace in our hearts.

EQUANIMITY (and Love)

Equanimity means showing calmness and composure in a difficult situation.

The word originates from the Latin *aequua* (meaning level or equal) and *animus* (meaning mind or soul). Thus equanimity means having a calm or level mental state, especially in the aftermath of a shock or disappointment.

Aequua is the clue, here. It guides us towards developing balance – cultivating a positive perspective when we are in a negative frame of mind. This leads to a state of calmness and serenity; ensuring that we are not thrown off course easily.

When we feel in this blissful state of taking life with a smile - riding its waves with confidence - we can't help but love the world, G-d and ourselves.

The point is not that everything has to be wonderful all of the time, for we are bound to face challenges (see both **faith** – Chapter One, and above). Indeed our life's work could be said to be to face those challenges with equanimity.

The Jewish people have faced several tough challenges in the past. Many have occurred during the Jewish months of *Tammuz* and *Av*. This is when we have *The Three Weeks* of lessened joy that include *Tisha B'Av* the saddest day in the Jewish calendar – a day on which many terrible things happened.

Both Jewish Temples were destroyed on *Tisha B'Av* (in different years). The 1st Temple was destroyed due to the three cardinal sins of idol worship, murder and immorality. Yet it was only seventy years later that the 2nd Temple was able to be built.

This 2nd Temple, on the other hand, has now been destroyed for over two thousand years. The reason given by Jewish sources? Because of the causeless hatred - hatred without a reason – practised by the Jewish people themselves. Had they loved and honoured each other more, then the 2nd Temple - and that very real feeling of tangible Jewish spirituality which we miss so much – would still be around today.

Not caring enough to give honour and love to others was considered more serious by G-d than the three cardinal sins combined.

We, in this day and age, also need to honour, take care of and love both others and *ourselves*. It cannot be said often enough that if we love ourselves more, then we are much more likely to behave in a loving way towards other people.

How do we learn to love? According to Rabbi Yitzchak Sandler (formerly of *Aish UK)*, this involves focusing on the positive attributes of other people (and ourselves).

This is easier to do when we feel happy in our own skins. Having equanimity (accepting serenely that people and the world are not always perfect) helps us to forgive ourselves for our mistakes; as well as forgiving others for theirs. Peace of mind also enables us to forgive G-d for any perceived wrongdoing we may attribute to Him.

The fact is that everything that G-d does is really for the good; even if our all-too-human eyes often have difficulty in seeing that. It also helps to remember that G-d renews the world (as we assert every day in the blessings of the *Shema*) at every moment; thus our lives can change for the better in an instant.

Significantly, the *9th of Av*, the saddest day in the Jewish calendar, is when the Messiah, it is said, will be born. We can learn from this that even sadness has a spark of new growth.

Equanimity is accepting that whilst there will be ups and downs in life, we have the ability to see the good in every situation; in life, ourselves, others and G-d. Acquiring this precious soul-state will lead to us feeling and expressing love.

EQUANIMITY

Another word is peace of mind
Accepting everything we find
No matter whether good or bad;
Soul-strings stay calm when mind is sad

Or body has unwanted pain.....
Yet know that things be good again
Sun will come out, a song we'll sing
By doing *mitzvahs* - the right thing

Equanimity - what a word!
Purest theatre of absurd
Yet with it, essence of serene
Acceptance of all that has been

And all that is and soon will be.....
Defining equanimity

It's having patience, waiting joy
Recalling pleasures of small boy
Knowing that sometimes life will test
Yet may bring out our very best

So keep your eye well on the ball
As take your aim, stand straight and tall
Like surfer navigating wave;
Discovering bright light in cave

Accepting life has ups and downs
Sorrows and joys, smiles and frowns
Treating each one as helpful friend
Thence challenge soon be at an end!

Equanimity - what a word!
Purest theatre of absurd
Yet with it, essence of serene
Acceptance of all that has been

(Opaque past – present, soon will be
This defines equanimity)

And all that is, calm peace will be…..
Defining equanimity

NUMBER FOUR – EQUANIMITY

There were 4 exiles that the Jewish people had to go through before the coming of the Messiah; the Babylonian exile, the Persian exile, the Greek exile - and the Roman exile that we are still in. Please G-d may we soon experience messianic days of peace, joy and closeness to You.

The connection, here, with the soul-trait of equanimity is that even in exile - including any personal or psychological exile we may feel - we need to be able to ride the waves of that exile. Our soul must remain calm and steady so that we can bear any difficulties or emotional pain that we may encounter.

The fourth month of the Jewish year is *Tammuz*. (This corresponds to our fourth soul-trait of equanimity). On the seventeenth of that month begins three weeks of semi-mourning practices related to the destruction of the 1st and 2nd Temples. We have now been without a Temple for over two thousand years. The significance of this is that G-d's presence is hidden from us; the world is not ideal; our lives are not perfect.....

That is why we need to work on the soul-trait of equanimity. We need peace of mind; that quiet soul-centred feeling that accepts the fact that we shall have ups and downs in our day-to-day living - but that recognises that the downs will pass. By being (soul) centred we will then be able to withstand the rough and tumble - the rush and crumble of any challenges and tests that we may face. We shall remain calm because we have mastered the valuable soul-trait of equanimity.

Interestingly, the fast of the *Seventeenth of Tammuz* is known as one of the *4 Fasts* we observe that are connected to the destruction of the Temples (read more in my book *Kosher Happiness)*. So again we see that the number 4 is connected to these negative events – and their repercussions - that equanimity is a useful psychological antidote to.

Yet the number 4 also has positive connotations:

'The number 4 is the place in which existence finds expression. We have seen 3 as symbolic of the essential foundation necessary for building a permanent structure. We now require the medium wherein that foundation can be built. The perfect forum for this lies in the number 4.'

Jewish Wisdom in the Numbers

The place for that foundation to be built is deep within our psyche. The means is acquiring the soul-trait of equanimity.

THE INNER SECRET OF EQUANIMITY

My mum asked me to buy her some cooking oil at Waitrose. No problem at all. However, when I arrived at the supermarket, I realised that by delaying my purchase for two days, I could take advantage of a special offer - and save nearly three pounds off the usual price of four pounds fifty. Now that's a big saving! I phoned my mum and she said "OK, buy it in two days' time"; but then she changed her mind. How frustrating. I was trying to save her money, but she was adamant she wanted the oil immediately. So I ended up paying the dearer price.

'Equanimity' was the soul-trait I needed in that situation. The reality is that life has its ups and downs; not everything goes the way we may wish it to go. Equanimity teaches us to accept this truism.

Thinking about equanimity helped me see this after the event (regarding the cooking oil). I'm not sure, though, if it would have helped me beforehand; I was too focused on making a saving. What is the inner secret to equanimity that could ingrain peace of mind (equanimity) on my heart, I wondered?

Kosher Happiness explains how the fourth month of the Jewish year, *Tammuz* (that corresponds to our fourth soul-trait of equanimity) is related to positive perception; seeing things in a good light. One powerful way of achieving this is by looking at life through the lens of humour.

There was actually both a funny side and a learning point that evolved from this matter. My mum, unlike me, has a much more carefree attitude towards money. That's the learning point; maybe I should loosen up around the issue of finances, too. However, what would have helped me even more than this - was seeing the humour of the situation; looking at it through a mirthful lens.

There I was trying to get the best supermarket deal possible; earnestly wondering why the shop should benefit at my mum's expense. Yet my mum often couldn't care a fig about such things! "What's the point of me waiting two days for the oil, just to save a few pence? I need it now" she thinks.

Mum, you have a point - and let me add *vive la difference*. We are not all the same, so let's enjoy and laugh about our differences. We should realise this intellectually, of course, if we have learned about the soul-trait of equanimity. But it is laughing at the absurdity of life - and the amazing diversity of human beings – that is the priceless quality that will bring equanimity to our hearts. The inner secret of equanimity is positive perception (with a squeeze of humour).

The ability to look at things with a sense of humour is surely worth more than the potential savings on a bottle of cooking oil!

PSALM 97 – A PSALM INSPIRING EQUANIMITY

Light is planted for the righteous; and for the straight of heart, joy

(Verse 11)

Rabbi Pliskin explains how the above verse can remind us to utilise the ups and downs of life as opportunities to connect with G-d.

'The natural state of a human being is joy. Joy is a healthy state – is healthy for us spiritually, emotionally and physically. Lack of joy comes from thinking in ways that block your joy. Different people have different obstacles to their joy. It is easy to blame other people, circumstances, or situations for one's lack of joy, but the only reason that other people, circumstances and situations might cause a lack of joy is because of the way that one views those factors.

The one who views everything in his life as an integral part of his service to the Almighty, will experience joy in dealing with whatever arises. (He will say) "This, too, is part of my mission in this world." The one who is "straight of heart" finds meaning in everything that occurs. Life is full of joy.'

Rabbi Zelig Pliskin

Thus cultivating the soul-trait of equanimity will lead us to a life of joy!

Mindful visualisation for healing

Expressing joy in dealing with whatever arises - and displaying an inner calmness amongst the turbulence of life – is what equanimity is all about. Our fourth soul-state is aligned with *Tammuz* – the fourth month of the Jewish year. This month, according to the oldest book of Kabbalah, the *Sefer Yetzirah*, is connected to the way we look at things.

We are told by the prophet Zechariah that the fast of the *Seventeenth of Tammuz* will one day be a day of rejoicing.

Visualise yourself, in Messianic times, standing in the courtyard of the Third Temple; singing, feasting and rejoicing on the (now) festival of the *Seventeenth of Tammuz*. For a moment, you remember once fasting on this day many moons ago. Now, the pendulum has swung – as it does when we treat less favourable times with equanimity.

As you return to the marvellous Messianic times once more, you enjoy this musical feast to the full; you experience a sense of deep-seated happiness and joy.

CHAPTER 5 - THE SOUL TRAIT OF SILENCE

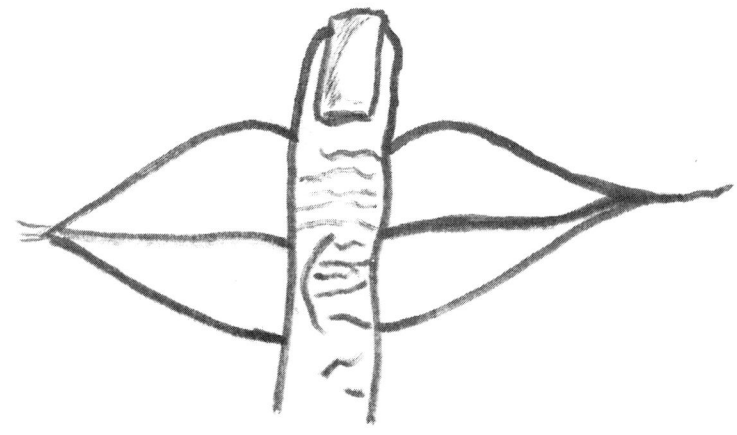

"Being silent allows inspiration and wisdom to enter"

SILENCE

Why should silence be one of our chosen soul-traits to cultivate? And even if we decide that it is important, surely it's very simple to achieve. We just close our mouths.

Shlomo Wolbe, in *Alei Shur,* disagrees. He states that: "Silence is a great skill, and by it you recognise the person of intelligence"

Ecclesiastes also indicates that there is value in silence. He says that "there is a time to be silent (and a time to speak)". Whilst the prophet Job, too, advises us to 'be silent and I will teach you wisdom.'

It is furthermore notable that the first word of our most well-known prayer, the *Shema,* urges us to hear.....to listen; and it is only by being silent that we are truly able to hear.

For example, if we are counselling someone or simply allowing a person to express themselves - then we need to be silent in order to be successful in our endeavours.

Speech, on the other hand, can be both creative and healing **and** destructive and dangerous. The sin of the spies - in giving an erroneous report regarding the potential of conquering the land of Israel - led to long-lasting consequences for the Jewish people. It is the root of the *Ninth of Av* (the Jewish date when this happened) becoming a fast day and the saddest day in the Jewish calendar.

One of the principal reasons given for the destruction of the 2nd Temple was because of the sin of *lashon hara* (slanderous speech or gossip) which is said, in our teachings, to be worse than murder, adultery and idol worship combined.

For whilst it was those three things that led to the destruction of the 1st Temple, this was rebuilt after a relatively short period of seventy years. The 2nd Temple, however, has still not been restored to us after more than two thousand years. Thus we can see that the effects of *lashon hara* are enormous. Surely keeping *shtum* (silent) is better and less harmful!

In addition, as Alan Morinis points out, 'certain sorts of insights and understandings about life...don't come by talking or even thinking - but are gifts of silence.'

To be aware of the so-called still small voice (of G-d), we need silence to be able to hear it. According to Maimonides (the *Rambam*), for example, the prophets of old (excepting *Moses*) had to be in a silent state - asleep or dreaming - in order to receive a prophecy. I quote from chabad.org:

'They receive prophetic visions only in a visionary dream or during the day after slumber has overtaken them, as the verse states: "I make Myself known to him in a vision. I speak to him in a dream." (*Numbers* 12:6).'

Rabbi Nachman of Breslov recommends silent contemplation *(hitbodedut)* as good practice. It is certainly true that expressing our thoughts and innermost desires to G-d can more easily follow after a period of meditative silence.

Alan Morinis gives us further counsel regarding silence. He advises: 'unless the words you are about to speak are absolutely necessary, remain silent.'

Rabbi Eliezer Papo extols the benefits of silence in relation to us mastering our anger. He states: 'Silence to anger is like water to fire.'

Another advantage of silence (and in particular silent contemplation) is that it offers us the chance to get to know ourselves better. As the Mussar great of the last generation, Rabbi Shlomo Wolbe, writes:

'You can only get a feeling for your internal life when you are alone. With a half hour of being alone you can come to feel things you never knew about yourself and see what you are lacking in spirituality. You will set new goals to reach.

This can only be done if you spend time alone in seclusion *(hitbodedut)* for half an hour. In this way you can start to build your internal, spiritual world.'

What may hinder us from achieving a state of silence? Alan Morinis says that it could be a lack of **humility** (see Chapter Six). He states: 'It's well recognised that arrogance is a huge obstacle to listening to what others have to say.' He also advises us (in the name of Rav Yechezekiel Levenstein) that in order to truly perceive a message (in our silence) we must contemplate it deeply.

Further guidance comes from Kabbalah in the form of *Adir BaMarom* by the *Ramchal* (as quoted in the book *Kabbalah* by Avraham Yaakov Finkel):

'You should be aware that the *yetzer hara* (evil inclination) takes hold of a person's body. But it cannot invade the body until it receives permission to enter. It obtains permission when the person's mouth utters shameful things. Surely the mouth is the gateway to the body. It is the only way the *yetzer hara* can enter.'

As the same book reminds us:

'Rabbi Shimon ben Gamliel said: I found nothing better for a person than silence.

(Avos - Ethics of the Fathers - 1:14)'

SILENCE (and Love)

You may remember the old story of two young people, out for a meal, chatting endlessly to one another. They are girlfriend and boyfriend trying to impress - or 'in love' perhaps.

Sitting at an adjoining table are an older couple. An odd word is said, here and there, but much of their time is spent sitting in silence. They have been married for so many years that they can practically read each other's thoughts. They love each other dearly and feel ever-so-comfortable in their own skins.

Many people, though, find it hard to be in their own company - let alone to be in near silence with someone else. For them, silence is a type of curse. Yet when we learn to love and accept ourselves for who we are, silence is one of life's greatest spiritual blessings.

Silence - when used in the right way - can actually engender love for ourselves.

By allowing ourselves a period of silent, calm reflection, we can re-evaluate our day, our month and our lives. This contemplation allows us to accept and celebrate our uniqueness whilst asserting our desire to realise our potential and become better people. I personally do this 'accounting of the soul' every Friday night – walking home from my *Shabbat* meal at my mum's.

The central prayer of our *davening* (praying) is the *shemoneh esereh*. This is also known as the *amidah* - which means the standing prayer. It is said in near silence and we actually whisper it to ourselves. This is an especially appropriate time for us to ask G-d for what we want in life. Yet, more than this, it is a time for us to assess what we truly need.

There are other benefits to silence.

Silence allows us to think before we speak; to pause in an ever-running world. Instead of being quick to criticise ourselves or others, we can utilise silence as a healing tool to allow us some moments to stop and reconsider.

Looking at a beautiful painting or natural scenery - in silence - is another health-giving measure that allows time for reflection and contemplation.

A brief period of silence allows us to appreciate G-d's many blessings.

Moreover, silence recognises what's really important in life and allows love to emerge.

Our matriarch Rachel showed this when she found out that her beloved husband-to-be (Jacob) had been deceived – and was going to marry her sister Leah in place of her. (Leah was covered up so Jacob wouldn't realise his mistake until after the ceremony).

Rachel both demonstrated her love and honour for Leah by not embarrassing her and staying silent. Instead of telling Jacob, she allowed this trickery, arranged by her father Lavan, to take place.

"When I gaze into your eyes in silence and appreciation - love appears."

SILENCE

Shhh!

Before the world was created
Was there silence?

Is an empty page
   an empty space

full of silence?

When imagining silence

sense I

beautifully transformed

Butterfly

Or see waves rolling.....roaring.....

an old silent film

Neither hearing

a jot

nor spot

of rain

Perhaps silence is a sound

soft resonance

of rustling leaves
            in lightest wind.

A peaceful mind

no *lashon hara*

anger stilled…..

Solely listening

white snow glistening

True love is silence

Two staring
into each other's eyes

An owl perched high.....gazing......

Silence is white

Giving others space

G-d is silence

A still small voice
yet thunder too

Silence of prayer
being a Jew

An idea plucked from gates of dawn

Inspiration.....

.....moment reborn

NUMBER FIVE - SILENCE

The fifth letter of the Hebrew alphabet is the letter *hay*. When found at the end of a word, this letter is silent. When used at the beginning of a word, the letter sounds like a gust of wind or the near silent breath of the soul.

In this respect, the letter *hay* signifies the moment of silence before speech begins - or after it ends.

'All speech begins with the 5th letter, *hay*, whose phonetic sound (huh) is associated with the exhalation of breath that precedes man's verbalising any speech.'

Jewish Wisdom in the Numbers

The connection between silence and speech is one that is worth examining. Let us first look at speech.

Jewish Wisdom in the Numbers explains:

'A (similar) metaphor of revelation is found in speech, where man reveals his inner essence by outwardly verbalising his innermost thoughts. In the giving of Torah at Sinai, there was a 5-fold mention of the word *kol* (voice). This finds broader expression in the record of how several Talmudic scholars (e.g., Rabbi Akiva, Rabbi Yochanan ben Zakkai, Rabbi Yehudah ben Bava) each had 5 primary disciples. These students were active in the process of expounding the Torah teachings of their master - in other words, the revelation of Torah through speech.'

From this we can see how the number 5 is related to speech. Now let us explore its relationship with silence.

It is interesting that the only *Yahrzeit* (anniversary of death) specifically mentioned in the Torah is that of Moses's brother Aaron on the first of *Av* - which is the fifth month of the Jewish year. Aaron has a particular connection with silence as we can see from the following, written by Dr Tali Loewenthal on chabad.org.

'At the moment of the final consecration of the Sanctuary, two of Aaron's sons were killed. Without consulting Moses, they let themselves be overcome by their enthusiasm and had come too close to the infinite power of the divine which was revealed in the Holy of Holies. In effect, they died as a result of their own unbridled ecstasy.

The Torah portion describes how Moses comforted Aaron, and that Aaron accepted what had happened: "And Aaron was silent" (Leviticus 10:3).

The power to be silent at certain moments of life and of history is an important strength. It expresses the awareness that G-d is infinite, and cannot be encapsulated in our human conceptions of what should take place.

Language, speech, signifies comprehensibility. Melody is beyond language, expressing moods which words cannot describe; and silence is yet higher.

The Talmud tells of a case when Moses himself was told by G-d to be silent. G-d showed him, in a vision, all future generations of the Jewish people, and the leaders of each generation. Moses was greatly impressed by the wisdom of Rabbi Akiva. Then he saw the way the Romans tortured him to death. "Is this the reward of his Torah knowledge?" Moses asked. G-d answered: "Be silent; thus it arose in My thought."

Before the event, assuming that there is some warning, one must do everything possible to prevent tragedy. Once it has happened, though, through our spiritual "silence" we reach a special closeness to the divine. Rashi tells us that because Aaron was silent, he was rewarded by G-d speaking directly to him later in the *Parshah* (portion of *Torah).*

However, this silence is only in terms of our intimate, personal relationship with G-d. In terms of our practical lives, even the worst and most horrific event is a call to action. It may be a call to do all one can to alleviate the suffering which has been caused. It may be a call to rebuild homes which have been lost. Or it may be a call to "rebuild" in a more spiritual way.

The Jewish people have confronted a physical Holocaust, and also various forms of spiritual damage through intermarriage and assimilation. How do we respond to this? Not through passive silence, however mystical that might be; but with supreme effort, action and joy, through which we try to help every Jew turn towards their Jewish heritage and rebuild Jewish family life and Jewish knowledge, around the globe.

Today, as Jews, we also face onslaught in Israel and elsewhere, through political action, media attacks and also sickening violence. Here, not silence, but the right voice defending Israel's right to exist is required: to exist healthily, with secure borders.

So we see that in the case of any kind of tragedy, G-d forbid, there is a time for "silence" like that of Aaron, yet there is also a call to respond, through action, love and determination, and thus to rebuild a shattered world. Through this we too, like Aaron, will merit divine revelation. G-d will bring the Messiah, rebuild the Temple in Jerusalem, and bring everlasting peace to the world.'

Another event that took place in the fifth month of *Av* - on *Tisha B'Av (the 9th of Av)* - was the outbreak of the 1st World War. Historically, we know that this was a major cause of the 2nd World War and the Holocaust. Rabbi Akiva Tatz tells of how it took a long time before many of the survivors of the Holocaust were able to speak out. He explains that their horror was so great that they simply weren't able to talk about what they had seen. This fits in with the idea that silence can express incomprehensibility.

However, there are also many stories of Holocaust survivors who went on to achieve incredible things after their 'moments of silence' had elapsed.

What is important for us, as Jews, is to study the *Chumash* (the 5 Books of Moses) – whether in silence or using speech (hearing a lecture or studying with a partner). This is our guidebook to living both meaningfully and with joy.

THE INNER SECRET OF SILENCE

Sometimes we feel so overwhelmed by things that we wonder how we can cope. We may worry overmuch about our health; or have a fear of having little breath and fainting. When Johnny gets like this (thankfully not too often) he thinks that he is probably having a panic attack.

He sometimes experiences this on a Friday night when he's *davening* in *shul* (praying in the synagogue). He says it seems to happen when he is singing along to the prayers. What is his response? To sing less rousingly or instead to mouth the psalms instead of voicing them. In such an instance, this is his version of being silent.

Similarly, when he is feeling stressed out, he doesn't say much; or chooses to speak in a soft low steady tone. This is another version of silence (turning the volume down).

When we are faced with a challenging situation, such as being in a difficult conversation with a person or organisation, it is sometimes best to remain silent; letting the other person exhaust what they want to say before giving our response.

So silence, or turning down the volume, can be seen to have its merits. Yet silence per se can sometimes seem a bit inactive; as if we are doing nothing. Is silence really enough *by itself* to effect positive change?

Silence is our fifth soul-trait; corresponding to *Av,* the fifth Jewish month of the year. The special kabbalistic sense of this month is correct *hearing* or *listening* (see *Kosher Happiness*).

This gives a clue to the inner secret of silence – the ability to listen.

Truly hearing what the other person is saying. Listening to what our body is telling us. Hearing what is going on inside of us emotionally. By doing these, silence becomes a pro-active soul-trait that can cause transformation.

Silence is truly golden when we ally it to listening. For example, when I take the half an hour walk back from my mum to my home on a Friday night, I take the advice of Rabbi Yisroel Roll. *In silence*, I mentally go through each day of the previous week - recalling its events, what I did and what I thought. I am listening to myself in mindful contemplation.

Try it for yourself - just once a week. Examine your actions and listen to your thoughts whilst experiencing the wonderful benefits of silence.

PSALM 23 – A PSALM INPIRING SILENCE

Though I walk in the valley overshadowed by death, I will fear no evil, for You are with me

(Verse 4)

'"For you are with me." What is the difference between just repeating these words of Psalms, and actually experiencing them? It is the difference between living life with inner peace and tranquillity, and living life with anxiety and despair. It is the difference between feeling a sense of togetherness and oneness with the Creator and Sustainer of the entire universe, and feeling alone and lonesome. It is the difference between constantly feeling a sense of meaning and purpose, and feeling a sense of emptiness and futility.

"For You are with me." What does this mean? It means that you are aware that *Hashem (G-d)* is with you in the most challenging times and the most deserted places.....when you celebrate and when you grieve.....when you are ill or hurt.....when you are healthy and vibrant.'

Rabbi Zelig Pliskin

When we are challenged in our lives, we often suffer in silence. Yet silence, as we have indicated in this chapter, can be a wonderful aid to healing. Especially when we walk in the fresh air and discover clarity - inspired by nature's surroundings.

Remember that being silent allows wisdom and inspiration to enter.

But not necessarily when we feel alone.

Yes, when we feel particularly vulnerable, we often need to listen to ourselves, to others and to G-d. But we also need to **speak** to someone to 'talk it over' – and who better to talk to than G-d?

Talk to G-d and then become silent for a few moments – awaiting a message from Him to enter your consciousness.

Mindful visualisation for healing

Visualise yourself at your most vulnerable and questioning.

Imagine a time in the past when you were, metaphorically, walking in a valley overshadowed by death, disease or despair. At least, that is how it felt – without hope.....hopeless.

Now imagine yourself, sometime in the future, in a happy, joyous moment. You are smiling and relaxed. Your past trials ended many moons ago. What was it that helped you escape from 'death valley'? Was it a friendly word, a flash of inspiration, a moment of insight, talking to G-d or a family member.....or did your fears or challenges evaporate by themselves in a silent puff of smoke?

How did G-d help you?

Now imagine that you have a minor challenge to deal with. See yourself saying out loud, and with belief, several times:

"I will fear no evil, for You (G-d) are with me."

Then relax your body, allow your shoulders to drop, breathe deeply and let out a sigh.

Be silent; remember (or imagine) a time of inner peace - experience and enjoy it NOW.

CHAPTER 6 - THE SOUL TRAIT OF HUMILITY

"Humility recognises our strengths and weaknesses as gifts of G-d"

HUMILITY

Humility is simply being aware of our own virtues (and faults) - and the virtues and abilities of others too; whilst recognising that all are gifts of G-d.

Alan Morinis tells us that:

'Humility is not an extreme quality, but rather a balanced, moderate, accurate understanding of yourself that you act on in your life.

Rabbi Abraham Isaac Cook makes the point that being humble shouldn't bring us down - in fact it should do the exact opposite! He states:

"When humility affects depression, it is defective: when it is genuine, it inspires joy, courage, and inner dignity."

So being humble is being real. It also goes hand-in-hand with self-esteem because it recognises our virtues. Moses was known as being the humblest man on earth. Yet he was a great leader - because he knew his strengths and used them.'

Humility is thus about occupying our rightful space.

Let us repeat Alan Morinis's example of a police officer - from his excellent book *Everyday Holiness*. He explains how police officers occupy a large space when directing traffic. Yet they take up a much smaller one when their role is as a parent at a parent-teachers night.

Humility is a vital soul-trait to develop. Morinis reminds us that 'Not only can one not take credit for the blessings that show up in one's life, but those blessings are actually not gifts as much as **obligations**......One who is wealthy must help those in need.....One who is strong must help the weak and rescue the oppressed......You are meant to play a unique role in life, and that role has dimensionality that is yours to occupy. A key aspect of wisdom is to know who you are and where you fit into greater schemes'.

What G-d given gifts do *you* have that may be used to benefit others? Can your height help someone by you handing them an item on a high shelf in a supermarket? Can your car be used to give someone a lift?

Orchot Tzaddikim (The Ways of the Righteous) states that a small deed done in humility is one thousand times more acceptable to G-d than a great deed done in pride.

For me, humility is represented by the tiny *yud* (the Hebrew letter connected to the sixth Jewish month of *Elul* - see my book *Kosher Happiness*). It is both small (in size) and great in that it is found in G-d's name *Hashem (Yud, Keh, Vov, Keh).*

Humility is thus being aware of both our smallness and our greatness. It is both the 'me' that is dust and ashes and the 'me' that is a child of G-d.

Thus we must not get too puffed up in pride. As Alan Morinis says:

'Being egotistical is not *like* idolatry: it *is* idolatry. And humility is the antidote.....Indeed a humble person can be defined as someone who does not take credit for what he or she has done, because the humble person is well aware of being the recipient of gifts from other people and G-d. (Whether it be) intelligence, strength, perseverance, sensitivity, awareness..... (Yet) we can take credit for our ethical choices. If when faced with a dilemma or a temptation, I make a choice for the good (or bad!) the credit is mine.'

As Judaism (Berachot 33b) teaches us "Everything is in the hands of heaven except for the fear of heaven." (I.e. our own ethical/spiritual choices are totally under our control – even if what happens to us is not).

Yet without being aware of our greatness - we can also not be truly humble.

'One who denies one's strengths is not humble (because) all his strengths and accomplishments are a gift from heaven.'

(Rabbi Leib Chasman)

Morinis teaches us one way of achieving humility:

'To practise humility, never be the first to speak. Alternatively, to stretch into your space, speak up more readily.'

It is also a great idea to find someone who can point out and encourage our strengths.

Humble or Bumble!

I raced into my local library in order to secure a computer where I could work on both this chapter and the previous one. I noticed one computer free and asked the librarian to book me onto it. She explained that the computer booking service wasn't working. A moment later an elderly woman sat down in 'my' seat and managed to book herself on 'my' computer. I complained to the librarian - as I thought it was her fault that I had been usurped by this other person.

The librarian and I found ourselves standing over the offending computer discussing this matter. Then the elderly woman calmly intervened and said that she wasn't that concerned about using the computer anyway – and she graciously logged off, allowing me to use it.

Victory? No way. Here I was about to write about the merits of humility, whilst behaving in an utterly selfish way! OK, so I didn't ask the woman to vacate the computer; she willingly did that herself. She possibly didn't really care about using it. Nevertheless, I should have been humble and 'known my place.' I should have waited for the next computer to become available. I should have remembered that **equanimity** (see Chapter Four) means accepting that things in life will not always go our way.

Humility means making space for another – as we are no more important than they are. The clue to how I should have behaved is in Chapter Five. I should have displayed silence rather than hubris.

You may wonder why I entitled this shameful story 'humble or bumble.'

Let me explain. I exhibited less than perfect behaviour; unfortunately we all do so sometimes. Nevertheless, however much we may wish to improve on our soul-traits, we don't want to beat ourselves up when we fall short. It is counter- productive.

'Humble or bumble' is a much more friendly way of referring to our errors than, for example, "I wasn't humble, I was selfish." The words we use (even and especially to ourselves) really matter. 'Humble or bumble' is a phrase we can use to rebuke ourselves in a more gentle and kindly manner; this friendly reproach will hopefully encourage us towards more positive results in the future.

HUMILITY (and Love)

When we are truly humble, we appreciate all the gifts and abilities that G-d has given us. We then wish, in return, to use them for the benefit of Humankind. We begin to be grateful and to love the unique person we are.

When we are truly humble, we become aware of the gifts that G-d has given to other people. We allow them the space they need to express themselves; to be themselves and to do their own thing. We begin to love them for who they are.

We appreciate our weaknesses, too, and know that we must do the best we can to rectify them and to become the best person we can be.

Humility means that we also accept that other people have their weaknesses. Humility, in fact, is about acceptance. So we must try to be accepting when other people go astray or are unable to act in the same way that we would have acted (or would have liked to have acted).

The initials of the sixth Jewish month of *Elul* - which corresponds to our sixth soul-trait of humility - are *Aleph, Lamed, Vov, Lamed*. These letters stand for the phrase (from the biblical *Song of Songs*): *Ani L'dodi V'dodi Li*, which means "I am to my beloved and my beloved is to me." This gives us a clue that *Elul* is connected to love.

Elul is the month when *chassidus* says that 'The King is in the Field.' (*Chassidus* is the movement within Judaism founded by Rabbi Yisrael Ba'al Shem Tov 1698-1760 CE).

This, *chassidus* explains, is when G-d (the King) comes to meet us - at our earthly level – giving us the opportunity to welcome Him and relate to Him as a friend. In similar fashion, we should stretch out our hands and welcome others as our friend. (In the next month of *Tishrei,* the month of the Jewish New Year, we traditionally honour G-d as our King rather than our friend or father).

Elul is notably the month of preparation for the Jewish High Holy Days of *Rosh Hashana* (the New Year) and *Yom Kippur* (the Day of Atonement). What better preparation for them could there be than loving ourselves and others more? When we do so, we 'wipe our slate clean' and are able to start the New Year in a pure and joyful state.

By having humility, we realise that G-d created us and thus we – and others - are a part or spark of G-d.

This means that we can achieve great things and relate to people in an extraordinary way - if only we knew it. Additionally, we can improve our own soul-traits to an amazing level. We also have the capacity to give and receive endless amounts of love.

G-d has made us creatures of love; filled with love.

(What is *chassidus?* One description that I like is given by Rabbi Tsvi Freeman, a senior editor at chabad.org. He explains that:

'The Chassidic movement taught Jews to serve G-d with love and joy rather than fear and trembling, to sing and dance rather than cry and fast. What concerns G-d the most, the Baal Shem Tov would preach, is that you serve Him with your heart. Love G-d, even if you don't always understand His ways; love His Torah, even if you can barely read the words; and most of all, love one another, even if that "other" doesn't measure up to the expectations of G-d and His Torah. And celebrate all of the above.)'

HUMILITY

Humility sounds like humble
When said in flirty mumble
And yet it's nothing of the kind
So on this fact don't stumble

Humility knows well its place
Gives you and I our unique space
When it's your turn to speak your mind
I run without a trace!

Humility says "I am great"
In some skill-sets, at any rate
It's not afraid to take the lead
Or wonders to create

Humility admits it's small
A baby always on the crawl
Yet when opportunities seed
It goes and conquers all

Humility, Moshe had that
He led the Jews in desert flat
(Clouds protected them from the sun)
He knew where life was at

Humility gives thanks to G-d
As source of genius and odd
Giant and tiny all in one
Somewhat of a strange bod!

Humility is me and you
Respecting atheist and Jew
(Five minutes of fame's very well......)
Shines light upon what's true

Humility - it's your turn now
To point out how to whoop and wow
But when it's my place to excel
I'll show everyone how!

(It's living in the now)

NUMBER SIX - HUMILITY

Our sixth soul-trait, humility, has two sides to it. It is both about recognising our limitations - and also being aware of our exceptional G-d given talents. In this day and age, it is probably the latter that needs more work.

The number 6 reminds us of the 6 dimensions of the world - 6 dimensional space. Left, right, up, down, forwards and backwards. In fact, the very 6 directions that we wave our palm-branch *(lulav)* on the joyous Jewish harvest festival of *Succot.* One reason we do this is to remind us that G-d is everywhere. Yet it can also remind us that our talents, once recognised, can stretch much further than we ever thought they could. We need to be truly humble to be aware of this.

Jewish Wisdom in the Numbers puts it another way:
'Due to the fact that there are 6 all-encompassing sides in the natural world, this number stands as the epitome of *gashmiyus,* corporeality (physicality). That ability to incorporate all sides and directions on Earth means that 6 is the number used to denote the attainment of *sheleimus,* completion, in the physical realm. Here it reaches a state of completeness in its ability to fully represent the expression of reality within the natural world.'

The reality is that we are both tiny in regards to *Hashem* (G-d) and of great potential, being children of G-d.

The sixth day, in fact, was when man was created - and the sixth day of the Jewish month of *Sivan* is the festival of *Shavuot* that celebrates the giving of the holy *Torah.* These two facts remind us that mankind are children of G-d. Also that man has a wonderful source of learning about personality development; from none other than G-d's character traits as described in the *Torah.*

If humility is all about 'occupying our rightful space' (as discussed earlier on in the chapter), we should thus be aware of our potential and very real greatness which can and must be used for the betterment of the world.

In Kabbalah, we learn that *Elul,* the sixth month of the Jewish Year, has a correspondence with the Hebrew letter *yud.* This is the smallest letter of the Hebrew alphabet; yet it is also included in G-d's name *Hashem.* This reminds us of how small (and great) we are - and also of the fact that we should never fail to acknowledge the greatness of others (and G-d, of course).

From the above we can see that the number 6, therefore, connects to humility; by suggesting to us that we 'know and occupy our place' in this world…..by recognising both our smallness and our greatness!

THE INNER SECRET OF HUMILITY

Rebecca only got to see the letter threatening to reduce her wages, a short time before *Shabbat* (the restful Jewish Sabbath - when amongst other things all technology is forbidden). She needed to prepare for the Sabbath, but she was spooked by the letter of foreboding.

If she did nothing now, she would have to wait the three days until Monday before taking action; leaving a whole weekend of worry. She therefore made a couple of immediate but brief phone calls. These established that things might not be as bad as she first thought. She now decided she could wait until Tuesday before taking any more potential action.

Surely this is, in essence, one aspect of humility; recognising how much we can do at any one particular time. Rebecca decided that there was nothing she could do on the non-working English weekend. Thus she realised that it was worth waiting until the following Tuesday - when her boss had promised to clarify the situation. She would then know for sure whether she needed to take any further action - based on fact.

However, Rebecca still felt a little stressed. She needed something more to calm and reassure her - the veritable inner secret of humility. Except that, at that point, she wasn't quite sure what it was.

So she carried on doing the things she had to. On *Shabbat* morning she went to *daven* in *shul* (attend a prayer service) and the following day she went to visit her mum in hospital. Making our own unique contribution is one major aspect of showing humility.

Rebecca had chatted to a friend after *Shabbat* prayers and this lightened her mood somewhat. It helped her to realise that her decision to delay any further action until she had spoken with her boss the following Tuesday was the right one. She felt calmer, now - and I think she'd discovered the inner secret to humility in the process.

"Take control! Set your own agenda; your own time-scale."

By coming to the awareness that she had taken control - by making a choice as to when she needed to embark on potential further action - Rebecca felt more in charge of things; resulting in her stress dissipating.

Humility is recognising our own talents (which are a gift from G-d) and using them when they are needed. The inner secret of humility is to take control by deciding *when* to act.

The sixth month of the Jewish year is *Elul*. Its special soul-sense according to the *Sefer Yetzirah* - the oldest book in *Kabbalah* - is correct action. (See *Kosher Happiness* for more).

We can boost our soul-trait of humility by taking control - choosing when to act – and living our life productively in the meantime.

'Action' is the inner secret of humility.

PSALM 8 – A PSALM INSPIRING HUMILITY

What is frail man that You should remember him, and the son of mortal man that you should be mindful of him?

(Verse 5)

Yet, You have made him but slightly less than the angels, and crowned him with soul and splendour

(Verse 6)

You give him dominion over Your handiwork. You placed everything under his feet

(Verse 7)

'Without the value and power that our Creator has given us, we are nothing. We are (but) dust and ashes. With the value and power that is the gift to each one of us from our loving Father and King, Creator and Sustainer of the Universe, we are remarkable beings. The entire world was created for us.

This view of humanity can instil in us both humility and positive self-esteem. Our value is given to us by *Hashem (G-d)*, no human being can take it away. We do not need any mortal's approval or appreciation, to claim our value. It is a given.

There is no validity to boasting (either), since no matter what our accomplishments and positive attributes, we are still miniscule, limited, and only temporarily in this world.' Rabbi Pliskin describes perfectly what this soul-trait of humility is about. In this day and age, I would suggest that our main challenge (in humility) is to attain self-esteem rather than a feeling of smallness. Indeed, humility is both knowing our smallness - whilst also, and especially, recognising our greatness. So, if we are truly humble, we naturally have positive self-esteem.

Mindful visualisation for healing

Imagine yourself, for a moment, alone in the vast universe; of seas and mountains, stars and planets. Then think of the majesty of the almighty G-d who created all this. Perhaps you are Adam, the first being, in the wondrous Garden of Eden. You just know that you are a child of G-d.

Now visualise yourself as only slightly less than an angel. Your brain is much more powerful than you could possibly ever conceive. Contemplate the fact that Man has invented aeroplanes and cures for diseases. He has stepped on the moon and created great works of art and music....

Now, you decide, is the time for you to use *your* G-d given strengths and abilities to make a meaningful difference and improvement to the world.

You see yourself smiling at a neighbour and helping someone in need......knowing that this is what G-d created you for. To be the best person you can be and a help-mate to others; to be a living blessing in fact.

You feel good as you begin to engage with life with renewed excitement, purpose and passion.

CHAPTER 7 - THE SOUL TRAIT OF COMPASSION

"When I demonstrate compassion, it brings love and at-one-ment"

COMPASSION

'Compassion is one of the 13 traits attributed to the Holy One.....Just as one would want compassion in his time of need, so one should have compassion on others who are in need'

Orchot Tzaddikim (Ways of the Righteous)

I have a problem with this wise advice from *Ways of the Righteous.* Whilst I agree that we should aim to emulate

G-d's attributes - the problem is that we are not G-d! It is not (for example) so easy to be compassionate; to bring down this trait - which we know to be desirable - from our minds into our hearts.

Still, assuming we are in agreement with the above counsel from *Orchot Tzaddikim* (at least theoretically) let us stay with it, by examining what compassion is more deeply.

Compassion in Hebrew is *rachamim.* This comes from the root word *rechem* which means 'womb.'

This (says Alan Morinis) has led many commentators to link this soul-trait to the emotional bond a mother has with her child. Thus we should express compassion to someone - just as a loving mother would to her offspring.

Morinis adds that compassion emerges from an experience of being very, very close to another - or a *feeling* of closeness, or from an effort to draw closer to the other (to be almost at one with them).

Compassion happens (he says) when we are touched by someone's story or experience. To be touched is to have a physical connection...to join....to overcome any duality or separateness from another. Thus your sadness becomes my sadness and your joy becomes my joy. Morinis adds, most importantly, that loving others in our heart is not enough; we must express our love (and compassion) in deed as well.

Rambam (Maimonides) writes that a person can only love commensurate with the degree to which he or she *knows* the object of his or her love. And when we love someone, it is much easier for us to have compassion for them. So let us listen well to people in order to get to know them better. Once we have touched and been touched by a person emotionally, we will then find it easier to have compassion for them.

Touch is interestingly the special sense of the Jewish month of *Tishrei,* the seventh month of the year that corresponds to our seventh soul-trait of compassion. This month contains the festival of *Yom Kippur* - the holiest day of the year - when we feel closest to G-d and it seems that all of our souls touch. It is also a happy (if solemn) day on which we are forgiven for our sins and mistakes of the past year. A day on which, assuming we are genuine in our repentance, G-d has compassion for us. With our slate wiped clean, we can begin this Jewish New Year period with compassion

'Compassion has us believe that a person is inherently holy and has the capacity to change.' Alan Morinis is telling us that, when we are compassionate, we are judging a person favourably - according to his soul-nature (his *potential* to do and be good).

By having such a mind-set, we thus allow these ideas to seep into our hearts - enabling us to express compassion to everyone we meet. Furthermore, by regarding everyone as part of the *One* (or as a child of G-d) we will naturally wish to judge them with good grace and express compassion towards them.

Are there other practical measures we can take in order to feel compassion for another? Morinis advises identifying a person who may be in some physical or emotional pain; closing our eyes and visualising his or her experience from the inside as intensely as our mind will allow so that his/her pain will become our pain.

It may be also helpful to remember that *Yom Kippur* is the Day of Atonement. A play on words of 'atonement' is '**at-one**-ment.' Our aim is to feel at one with others – in order to be able to express compassion towards them more easily.

We must also express compassion towards ourselves; although this can be particularly difficult to do. Perhaps we need to repeatedly say to ourselves:

"I forgive myself for any and all mistakes I have made – whether intentional or unintentional."

A common psychological concept that I read long ago states that we always do what we think is for the best. Of course we all make mistakes. But having compassion for ourselves (and others) can help soften our negative judgement - and lead to the soothing acceptance that we are all only human, after all.

COMPASSION (and Love)

Love and compassion seem to go together like peas in a pod.

If we truly love someone (assuming it is real love and not infatuation) then we should feel and have compassion for them. We should be able to step into their shoes and see their world from their perspective.

If we have compassion for someone, though, does this necessarily mean that we love them?

I would argue perhaps yes. It may not be a romantic love; but being truly compassionate illustrates a deep caring that could be described as love.

Perhaps the clue to this is in the Hebrew word for love *ahava*. The root of the word is *hav* which means 'to give.'

Thus, the more we give to someone (this includes our time and attention) the more we love them. By giving of ourselves in an emotional way to someone - particularly by showing or feeling compassion for them - this engenders love. It is as though we have become at one with the other.

G-d is one. For example, He exhibits both attributes of judgement and loving-kindness. For our sakes, He errs on the side of *chesed* (loving-kindness) and shows compassion to us. If He acted out of strict judgment, on the other hand, we would all have a much shorter lifespan. We are all very much human and tend to make mistakes easily, which is why G-d needs to show compassion to us.

In Judaism a sin (*chet* in Hebrew) literally means 'to miss the mark' - like an archer might do as he aims for a bullseye. Even when trying to be moral and to obey G-d's commandments, we all often 'miss the mark.'

But G-d tinges his judgement with loving-kindness - thus His compassion and mercy are activated when we go off the *derech* (way). And every *Yom Kippur* (Day of Atonement) G-d grants us the opportunity to attain forgiveness for our mistakes.

In fact the *Talmud* (Oral Law) describes *Yom Kippur* as being the happiest day of the year (along with the minor festival of *Tu B'Av*).

The last Mishnah in the Tractate of Ta'anit states:

Rabbi Shimon ben Gamliel says, "There were never happier days for the Jews like the Fifteenth of Av and Yom Kippur; for on those days the daughters of Jerusalem would go out wearing borrowed white clothing so that they should not embarrass those who did not own such. These dresses required immersion in a mikvah (a bath or body of water used for the purpose of ritual immersion). The daughters of Jerusalem would go and dance in the vineyards and say, 'young man, lift up your eyes and see what you choose. Do not look for beauty, look for family - as it is stated in Proverbs (31) - grace is deceitful and beauty is vain, a woman that is G-d fearing is to be praised.'"

(Thanks to Nachum Mohl from jewishmag.com for the above quote).

The happiness, referred to above, is also due to G-d's compassion for us – that leads to Him granting us forgiveness.

Tu B'Av and *Yom Kippur* are, in fact, biblically connected. Whereas on *Tu B'Av* (the minor festival of the Fifteenth of Av), G-d forgave the sin of the spies; on *Yom Kippur*, He forgave the sin of the golden calf.

On every *Yom Kippur*, G-d similarly forgives us by showing us His attribute of compassion (assuming we have repented for going astray). Because G-d loves us, He forgives us.

Postscript

Just as G-d is one, so too is 'love!' The numerical value *(gematria)* of *ahava* (love) is thirteen.

The *gematria* for the number 'one' *(echod* in Hebrew) is also thirteen. This indicates that love equals oneness.

And by adding 'one' and 'love' together, we get twenty-six.

Twenty-six is the *gematria* of G-d's name *Hashem* - the very name of G-d that depicts mercy and compassion.

Let us all show love and compassion to ourselves (and others) too.

COMPASSION

On yourself be gentle
Deserve, thou, every good
Be calm, cool and collected
You really know you should!

Treat yourself with kid gloves
Smile whence make mistakes
Chances appear from errors
In films they do re-takes

Compassion, compassion

Never goes out of fashion

Just hug your inner child

Soothing words calm and mild

When the going gets tough
Feeling strong need to cry
Take yourself a breather fresh
Then give another try…..

Tell yourself "I'm a hero
That's why G-d gave me life"
Love yourself, it's easy as
Slicing with butter knife

Compassion, compassion

Never goes out of fashion

Just hug your inner child

Soothing words calm and mild

Remember when you were a kid
You dropped a plate - it broke
Your parents looked on lovingly
Treating it like a joke

Prey, mistakes don't matter!
Instead they're learning tools
Sins can be turned to *mitzvas*
Pebbles dropped into pools

Compassion, compassion

Never goes out of fashion

Just hug your inner child

Soothing words calm and mild

Just hug your inner child…..

NUMBER SEVEN - COMPASSION

'Jewish life is suffused with holiness. Not only is 7 the symbol of holiness; it is also the means of *how* to acquire that holiness.'

Jewish Wisdom in the Numbers

There's something special about the number 7. G-d created the world in six days and rested on the seventh. Thus He has granted us a most welcome and wonderful day of rest each week - the holy *Shabbat* (Sabbath). The Sabbath day is indeed so naturally infused with a restful holiness, that on this day we inherently act in a friendly way towards others; whilst displaying compassion to those who need it.

The seventh and most holy month of the Jewish year is *Tishrei*. This is because it is packed with more Jewish festivals than any other month. These include *Rosh Hashana* (the Jewish New Year), *Yom Kippur*, (the Day of Atonement) and the joyous festivals of *Succot* and *Simchat Torah*.

Interestingly, there are two major Jewish festivals of 7 days a-piece *Pesach* and *Succot* (although *Pesach* is observed for eight days outside of Israel). There is also a 7 week period between the festivals of *Pesach* and *Shavuot*. This is known as the *Omer* period during which we count all forty-nine (7x7) days; this is, in particular, a propitious time on which to work on our character traits.

Thus, we can see that the number 7 is connected to us both being and becoming holy.

How can we become even more holy, though? Judaism would advise that we keep the *mitzvot* (G-d given commandments), celebrate *Shabbat* and the Jewish festivals and also strive to become better and more kindly people.

One of the keys to becoming a better person is to work on the twelve soul-traits in this very book. Arguably, though, compassion is the premier soul-trait that is needed to become more holy.

If we wish to relate better and to help other people more - surely the ultimate holiness - we must learn to become more compassionate. When we are compassionate, we are able to help others much more easily than when, for example, we are annoyed with them!

We also need to be more compassionate with ourselves. When we do so, we naturally feel happier people; thus we are likely to be more responsive to the needs of others.

Yet, it is easy to become cross with ourselves or frustrated by our imperfect actions. This is when we especially need to treat ourselves with compassion and understand that it is only human for us to make mistakes. In fact, the very reason for G-d creating us is so that we can learn from our errors and improve our character. We must have faith in ourselves that we can achieve this.

As *Jewish Wisdom in the Numbers* reminds us:

'A righteous person falls 7 times - only to rise again.'

By having compassion for ourselves and others, we can become holy - which is all that G-d wishes of us.

THE INNER SECRET OF COMPASSION

Jack was a genuinely caring person. It was not much of a problem for him to feel sorry for someone less fortunate. Even if a rich person had lost a small amount of money, he would readily understand that he or she may be feeling a loss.

The person he found it hardest to have compassion for, though, was himself. This is perhaps not so surprising when we think how emotionally involved we are with ourselves. It is so easy for us to be hard on ourselves when we fail to live up to our own high standards and expectations.

Jack had a 'business' matter that should have been sorted out that morning but the person he had spoken to, whilst being pleasant, was quite useless. She promised, though, that a colleague "with more expertise" would be phoning him that very afternoon.

We are entitled to ask whether Jack should have had compassion for this 'quite useless woman.' Not necessarily. She wasn't qualified to deal with the matter in hand and so shouldn't have been the one to phone him in the first place.

(Although, it could be argued that if Jack was truly compassionate, he may have reasoned that she was just having a 'bad day').

Yet although Jack was cross with her, he realised, in hindsight, that he was really more annoyed with *himself* - for letting her end the conversation without resolving the issue.

He feels he can't do much more now except to feel annoyed and frustrated. Yet if he had had more compassion for himself, he wouldn't feel quite so bad. He would have reasoned that he is only human, after all.

Yet how does he conjure up such self-compassion? He knows it will do him good if he can. What Jack really needs to help him feel better is compassion's inner secret.

Basically, he needs to **relate** better to himself. He needs to love himself more, but, even more than that, he needs to be his own best friend.

The seventh month of the Jewish year (that connects to our seventh soul-trait of compassion) is *Tishrei;* it is packed with the festivals of *Rosh Hashana, Yom Kippur, Succot, Shemini Atzeret* and *Simchat Torah.* These are all concerned with our relationships; with others, G-d and our-selves. (See *Kosher Happiness* for more).

The special sense of this holy month is **touch**. To feel compassion, we must figuratively touch other people; reach out to them and try to understand their lives and the way they see the world.

But to feel compassion for ourselves, on the other hand, we may literally need to touch ourselves and perhaps give ourselves a hug.

We are so emotionally involved with ourselves, that it is that bit harder for us to give ourselves compassion. It's like counselling. It is much easier to counsel someone other than ourselves - because we are one step removed from the problematic situation. However empathetic we are, we can't feel someone's pain as much as they feel it themselves. So although we may understand their hurt and travails, we can examine their problem with clarity and distance – because we are not so emotionally affected.

Thus, when it comes to giving compassion or love to *ourselves*, we need to feel similarly calm and centred in order to distance ourselves from our own pain.

Let us try doing this by centring ourselves with the simple tool of energy healing. Just place the palms of your hands softly and slowly on the top of your head, then on the sides of your face, then on the front of your face, then on the back of your head - and so on, gradually covering every part of your body that you can comfortably reach. At the same time, say (or think) to yourself "I love myself, I forgive myself, I allow myself not to be perfect. When I show compassion to myself, it brings love and at-one-ment."

The important thing to remember is to allow your hands to remain on each part of your body for as long (or short) a time as you sense that part of your body needs comforting. (See more in my book *10 Days to Change your Life*).

The inner secret of compassion is touch.

PSALM 145 – A PSALM INSPIRING COMPASSION

Gracious and merciful is Hashem (G-d), slow to anger, and great in (bestowing) kindness.

Hashem is good to all; His mercies are on all His works

(Verses 8 and 9)

'The *Torah* (Jewish law) tells us to emulate *Hashem,* to walk in His ways. Just as *Hashem* is kind and merciful, we too need to develop these qualities within ourselves.

"*Hashem* is good to all." How can we be good to all? On a practical level, our resources are limited and finite. Our internal attitude, however, should be that we wish to do kindness to everyone we can. Our compassion and inner caring should encompass the entire world.

As you feel compassion, be aware that having this quality is a way in which you are emulating *Hashem.* Think of specific actions you can do, so that your compassion is translated into words and behaviour. When you read these verses (from Psalms) in the daily prayers, let them serve as a reminder to increase your acts of kindness to more people.

Rabbi Zelig Pliskin

Mindful visualisation for healing

We can use the power of atonement (which is the special gift granted us on the festival/fast of *Yom Kippur)* at any time of the year – in order to cleanse ourselves.

It becomes a priceless opportunity to ask our friends, family and G-d to show compassion and grant us forgiveness. (Ideally we will have asked our friends and family for forgiveness before the day of *Yom Kippur,* itself).

Breathe deeply and visualise yourself apologising to someone you have offended. Drop your shoulders and give a sigh of relief. Then imagine yourself praying to G-d; saying sorry for any transgressions you may have committed.

Now visualise yourself thoroughly cleansed from all past sins and mistakes.

See yourself infused with a ball of white light, entering and filling your body from head to toe. Now imagine this ball of white light becoming a sphere of loving energy and entering your body once again; this time infusing it with compassion, forgiveness and joy.

Now see yourself glowing - as a loving creation of G-d who was made to show compassion, share love and bring joy to the world.

Smile, drop your shoulders and feel good.

Now see yourself going out into the world and *doing* wonderful good deeds to others; speaking words of love, caring and compassion.

CHAPTER 8 - THE SOUL TRAIT OF TRUST

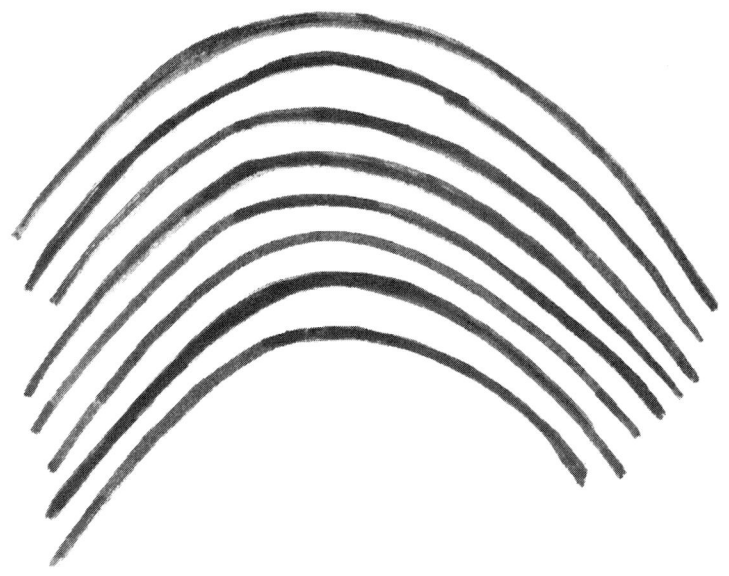

"When in doubt – say 'trust' aloud"

TRUST

If we agree that having faith is appreciating that everything happens for a reason decreed by G-d - see **faith** - Chapter One - then let us now see if we can tease out the difference between faith and trust.

Ramban (Nachmanides) says that faith can exist without trust; however it is impossible for trust to exist without faith.

So what is the difference between the two; and why do we need to achieve 'trust' if we already have faith that G-d exists?

As we alluded to in our discussion on *equanimity* in Chapter Four, 'everyone is subject to the slings and arrows of outrageous fortune' (to quote Alan Morinis). Thus we are bound to face problems and challenges in our lives. It is the norm. Yet what is also normal is for us to become stressed about even the smallest of things that may go wrong in our day to day living.

I think that having faith in G-d means that we intellectually understand that what is happening to us is the will of G-d. Yet we may still feel bothered about our situation. Having trust in G-d, on the other hand, is when we feel emotionally, in our bodies, that everything is and will be fine.

Rabbi Ibn Pakuda expounds on the enormous benefit of developing trust in G-d. He says that one who trusts in G-d "neither worries nor laments." He is "free of worldly cares and lives in security and tranquillity." He "is pleased with everything, even if it goes against his grain." As a servant of G-d, the challenges of life are just the stuff of a day's labour in the fields of the Lord.

Alan Morinis suggests that when worried we should recite "My life is in the hands of the One who made me."

Or, if we prefer, we could say the verse in Psalms (56:3) that states: "When I am afraid, I will put my trust in You."

Frumma Rosenberg-Gottlieb informs our discussion further. She explains:

'In a powerful affirmation that we quote in daily prayers, as well as in the Grace after Meals, the Prophet Jeremiah tells us that trust spawns certainty, and certainty breeds success: "*Baruch hagever asher yivtach baHashem v'hayah Hashem mivtacho* - Blessed is the man who trusts in G-d; G-d will be his security." Cultivating such trust is a lifelong project. It calls for making room in our awareness for a Higher Power, relying on G-d as the source of all challenges and blessings. It means acknowledging this Source regularly, learning about G-d and communicating with Him on a regular basis, keeping His number on speed dial on our metaphorical cell phones. This can be achieved through meditation and prayer.

For prayer to genuinely augment our trust and calm our souls, it must be mindful. Who is G-d? Why am I connecting to Him in this way? How can I enhance my awareness of His dynamic presence in the details of my daily life? Such a practice cultivates trust — and one who truly trusts in G-d's benevolent guidance will not be riddled with problems, nor with the gnawing feeling that something is lacking. Of course this doesn't mean life will be without challenges — as 3,800 years of Jewish history will readily attest! But our ability to cope with problems and follow through with effective solutions - increases in direct proportion to the calm certainty that comes with knowing G-d is our caring and capable partner.'

Alan Morinis gives us an exercise we can practise using the very same phrase that Rosenberg-Gottlieb quotes above. He teaches:

'Your assignment will require that you be equipped with a tool to help overcome fear. The tool is a phrase that appears in the Grace after Meals:

Baruch ha'gever asher yivtach b'Adonoy.

Blessed is the one who trusts in G-d.

Say this phrase a few times (now) until it is committed to memory, whether in Hebrew or in English. This will also serve as your morning affirmation key-phrase.

Next, identify something that you hold yourself back from doing - that is really not dangerous, but that you fear nevertheless. And now commit to doing that thing at least once each day, for this entire week.

For example, you may be reluctant to telephone a certain person because you fear the response you will receive. Maybe it is a person who you don't like to call because their mood is so unpredictable. Or someone who so likes to hear from you that you get trapped on the phone for hours.

Repeat the key-phrase to yourself several times then pick up the phone. You know it is the right thing to do, and you can trust G-d to make it work out just as it should.

Or maybe there are certain self-care tasks that you shy away from. You don't see your dentist as often as you should or, like I used to do, you appear at your doctor's office for an annual check-up about once every five years. Is it the fear of the pain, or denial of your mortality, that holds you back?

Repeat to yourself, "Blessed is the one who trusts in G-d," then pick up the phone and make an appointment. The fear is real, in that you feel it, but what happens when you offset your fear by trusting G-d?

Or, you might tend to be tight-fisted when it comes to giving charity, because who knows what lies ahead, and what if you find yourself in need in the months or years to come? Recognize that this is a fear as well. All that a person receives in a year is a matter of Divine decree. To short-change the present because of fear of what might lie in the future betrays a lack of trust.

Repeat to yourself "Blessed is the person who trusts in G-d." And then open your wallet to give more.

If one of these examples applies to you, you can make that your exercise for this period. If not, then find a similar pattern in your own life, where you are restrained from doing the right thing because of a fear, and where a reminder to trust will allow you to step forward.

In your Accounting of the Soul Diary, record your reluctance to act, how it felt to recite the phrase, how it felt to take the step of action, and (most importantly) what actually happened when you did. Was the fear warranted?

Even if the result was exactly as unpleasant as you thought would happen, could you handle it? What did you learn about your own inner traits through this exercise of crossing the distance between living in fear and living in trust?

When you record your observations, recognize that you have already begun to weave a web of trust in your heart. Now how does that feel?

Here's your key-phrase:

*"Baruch ha'gever asher yivtach b'Adonoy.
Blessed is the one who trusts in G-d."'*

Advice from Modern Day Psalms

In *Modern Day Psalms*, I devote a whole chapter to 'trust in G-d'. This is potentially the most important and vital of the soul-traits to work on. For when we let our worries dissolve, **knowing** that all is G-d's will and that all is for the best, we can then go forward to do good - and hopefully magnificent - things without inhibition.

The following exercise is taken from *Modern Day Psalms:*

'To strengthen your trust in G-d, recite the following verses from Psalm 27 with emotional energy:

*The Lord is my light and my salvation - whom then shall I fear?
The Lord is the stronghold of my life - of whom shall I be afraid?*

When evil men close in on me to devour my flesh, it is they, my enemies and foes, who stumble and fall.

(Verses One and Two)

Hope in the Lord; strengthen yourself and He will give you courage, and hope in the Lord!

(Verse Fourteen)

Doing such a practice is a favourite recommendation of mine. I first advise it in my book *10 Days to Change your Life* when discussing 'Affirmations.' However, I was not the first person to recommend this. Long ago, Rabbi Salanter, founder of the *Mussar* (Jewish Ethics) movement, encouraged his students to recite phrases that in some way related to the particular character trait they were working on at the time.

Alan Morinis in *Climbing Jacob's Ladder* puts it this way:

'The basic practice is to repeat the phrase over and over, for as long as it takes to shake it loose of the intellect so that it can carry its message directly to the heart. But simply saying the phrase is not enough. Rabbi Salanter insisted that the repetition be done aloud, with great emotion......"with lips aflame," to use his own words, and the name he gave this practice was *hitpa'alut,* meaning "with intense emotional excitement."'

TRUST (and Love)

Personally speaking, trust is the most important quality that I value - both as a friend and in a friend.

Trusting in ourselves, in fact, is an important component of loving ourselves; and vice versa. When we make mistakes or do the wrong thing, we need to trust that eventually we will do the right thing and make amends. If we don't love ourselves, it is harder for us to have this trust.

Trust can also lead to love.

If we trust G-d to help us on our way, we feel grateful to Him when good things happen to us; thus we come to love Him.

Trusting G-d also gives us confidence.

G-d has given us amazing talents as we discussed in Chapter Six - Humility. Our job is to trust in our unique abilities so that we can use them for the good of mankind. G-d has also given us the capability to love others and show compassion. We must trust in ourselves enough so as we can exhibit these qualities.

When Moses was due to come down from Mount Sinai with the Ten Commandments, the Jewish people miscalculated the day of his expected descent. Thus, in his absence, they built a golden calf as something they could put their spiritual focus upon. This led to lasting negative consequences for the Jewish people. The root of this was their lack of trust in G-d (and Moses).

Trust is the antithesis of doubt. If we trust, our fear lessens, we feel more relaxed - and we are able to love more.

I am in the middle of writing my fifth book. Although, in some ways it is a struggle, I trust myself to complete it. If my trust wavers, however, I may not do so. But where does this trust and confidence come from? From my past; the knowledge that I have already written four books helps an awful lot. We must continue to believe in ourselves - by working on the soul-trait of trust - using every means available.

The same applies to trusting in G-d. It was He who brought the world into existence and gave us life. G-d also redeemed and set free the Jewish people from Egypt. We thus owe it to ourselves to trust in Him to help us today - and to bring *Moshiach* (the Messiah) speedily in our days (please G-d).

Trust is faith in action. If faith is *believing* that everything will turn out fine, then trust is having the confidence to apply that faith and ensure that everything *will be* fine; taking positive action and doing our bit to repair and better the world.

Faith and love equal trust. Love is the positive emotion that gives fuel to the fire of faith. Loving others is the energy that motivates us to go take action and do good.

By loving and caring enough we will prevail.

TRUST

There's an answer, she said, to your question
(If you'd just let me make a suggestion)
Trust all will be well with your life
Propose and I may be your wife

If not, though, trust all will be better
In view of your kindly love letter
Experience put to good use;
Plying trust never needs an excuse

When you trust that things will be OK
Always ends up being a good day
In fact if you choose trust, just so
Perhaps I'll decide not to go!

You see it is working already
Can see from your stance you're more steady
Or is it with me you're nonplussed?
Nought's impossible when you have trust!

NUMBER EIGHT - TRUST

'We have seen how the number 7 corresponds to the 7 days of Creation, and by extension to the sanctification of the natural world. Its successor, the number 8, goes one stage further. It goes beyond - to reach a level that is higher than nature. The number 8 denotes "transcendence." It symbolises that a Jew is not subject to the natural realm. He has the ability to break free from This World and its limitations. He arises above that natural order.'

Jewish Wisdom in the Numbers

The above book adds that this can be seen from the respective Hebrew names of 7 and 8. Seven is *sheva* which is similar to *shovaa* (satisfaction) - the satisfaction one feels when he completes his worldly requirements. Whereas *shemona* (eight) relates to *shooman* (fat) which signifies having more than is necessary.

The number 8 in Judaism thus signifies the miraculous. It denotes that there is more to life than the normal or the necessary; that there is more to existence than we can physically see. This is illustrated, most famously, in the miracle of *Chanukah* (the festival of lights) when a small flask of pure oil - containing only enough oil for one day - miraculously burned for 8 days.

Often, in our lives, when things are seemingly going against us, we literally can't see the light. Everything appears bleak; we can't possibly envisage how things are going to work out - let alone be for the best.

If we have faith (see Chapter One) we may understand that we are in a challenging situation - for a reason decreed by G-d. Sometimes, we may comprehend a smidgen of that rationale, yet often we do not. Still, we may be comforted somewhat that whatever is happening – is happening for a reason; even if that reason is unknown to us.

In response, we may choose to improve on our character traits or do more *mitzvot* (Jewish laws and/or good things to others) in hope that G-d will see fit to better our situation in return. There is an idea in Judaism that by transforming ourselves into someone different – someone better – then G-d's judgment for us will change; because He is now judging a different person!

Yet, even if, by having faith, we may know in our mind that our 'suffering' has some purpose, we may not feel this enough in our bones to react in the best way possible. Worse, we may think that we have to 'suffer' or experience our bad situation - without any hope of a better life ahead.

This is where 'trust in G-d' comes in. If we have trust, we literally believe in the miraculous. We are not stuck in the mud or in our ancient (or modern-day) belief systems. We have G-d on our side. We believe miracles can happen.

Maybe tomorrow we will recover - despite what our physician has told us. Maybe we shall be married in three months, to a woman we are yet to meet. Maybe our financial situation will improve. Or we will receive an inheritance or a new job.

Haven't you ever experienced something good following something bad? A small-scale example I can give is when I was looking for a new CD player. I saw one in a charity shop that, on reflection, I thought was suitable. So I went back to the shop the next day to purchase it; but someone had beaten me to it. I was quite disappointed; yet just a couple of weeks later I found (and bought) a much better one - in the very same shop. So, I was (retrospectively) delighted that I hadn't managed to buy the first one that I saw!

'When a Jew falls, he picks himself up. "The righteous may fall seven times: he will arise" (*Proverbs 24:16*). It is upon the eighth occasion that he starts a new phase.'

Jewish Wisdom in the Numbers

This maxim applies to our negative *thoughts*, too. When we are able to disregard our previous beliefs and perceptions - that our current situation is beyond repair and beyond all hope - we have picked ourselves up and achieved our own minor miracle. We have reached the exalted state of *bitachon* - trust in G-d - that things will improve.

And once we have *bitachon,* our thoughts and actions will reflect that blissful state of stress-free living that - *bitachon* brings.

THE INNER SECRET OF TRUST

Obsession is a double-edged sword. On the one hand, it can be the driving force that takes us to success, whether in physical or spiritual matters. It can propel us to reach untold heights in business, for example; or, in the spiritual realm, to master the trait of, say, loving kindness.

However, there can also be some negative effects stemming from obsession.

Ian saw himself as a Robin Hood figure in a battle with a corrupt organisation. Working out the exact wording of the next letter he needed to write to them played on his mind over and over again. This began to stress him out. The same thing happened in relation to a female he wished he had chatted up. He acquired the bad habit of replaying the scene repeatedly in his mind; focusing on that exact moment he thought he had messed up.

These are the precise situations in which we need 'trust'.

Before the event, we need to trust in ourselves; that we can, and will, succeed in our endeavours. We need to try our very best and act as if the end result depends entirely upon us.

After the event, however, we need to let go of any anxiety and trust that the end result turned out exactly as G-d wished.

Yet trust is not such an easy soul-trait to develop. Even concerning things that we are good at or have a special talent in - we can suffer a dip in confidence and start to doubt ourselves.

As for trusting in G-d – however much we may desperately want to - it is often quite difficult. Especially when we focus on, what we consider to be, the bad in our lives - as opposed to the good.

So what is the inner secret of trust; the secret that will take our intellectual understanding of this trait deep within our hearts?

In the eighth month of the Jewish year, *Cheshvan* - the month that our eighth soul-trait corresponds to - there are no festivals at all. That is why the month is often called *Marcheshvan,* which means bitter *Cheshvan*. And that's sometimes how we feel - bitter or empty. Yet eight in Judaism also symbolises the miraculous (see above – Number Eight – Trust). So what is the secret to believing and trusting that, seemingly miraculously, everything will turn out for the good?

The special sense of *Cheshvan* gives us a clue; it is the sense of smell - the sense that involves us **breathing**.

Every morning, we thank G-d for returning our soul back to us and thus renewing our ongoing life-story. Surely, there can be no greater miracle than life itself; yet we automatically trust (almost without thinking) that G-d will reward us with another day of existence tomorrow.

Whatever challenges we may have in our lives, we just need to remember that we are still in the game - whether we seem to be winning or losing it. We need to remind ourselves that the sun will still rise tomorrow. Whatever our situation is, we can become mindful and enjoy and marvel at G-d's extraordinary handiwork. We can take a breath.....take a breather......stop and smell the roses - and learn to trust in ourselves and G-d once more.

With these positive thoughts in our mind, we can then become a breath of fresh air to everyone we know, encounter and love. (Under your breath just try whispering the word 'trust' and watch yourself relax).

By taking time out to focus on our breathing - or on really noticing and enjoying a favourite aroma…..our negative obsessions can disappear in a moment. Trust me!

PSALM 27 – A PSALM INSPIRING TRUST

Hope to Hashem (G-d). Be strong! Strengthen yourself and He will give you courage - and hope to Hashem

(Verse 14)

'What is the root element of having hope in *Hashem?* You realise that He is the very essence of kindness and compassion. You realise that He loves you on the deepest level possible. You realise that He is all-powerful and has the ability to help you. So your having this hope, is making a powerful statement of your basic belief and trust in *Hashem.* Thinking the thoughts of hope to *Hashem* is spiritually and emotionally life-enhancing.'

Rabbi Zelig Pliskin

Saying these thoughts out loud will be even more powerful. Similarly, whenever you are feeling doubt, take a deep breath; allow yourself a sigh and let your shoulders drop; then say "trust" (followed by the verse from Psalms above) aloud!

Mindful visualisation for healing

This eighth soul-trait of 'trust' corresponds to the eighth month of the Jewish year, *Cheshvan*.

This month is also known as *Marcheshvan* which means bitter *Cheshvan*. One reason for this is that it is the only Jewish month without any festival or fast to help guide us in our Jewish spiritual and personal growth. However, *Cheshvan* is also notably the month when it is said that the long-awaited Third Temple will be built. This will be a propitious time when G-d's presence will be clearly felt.

Now visualise yourself feeling calm and happy in the absolute certainty that messianic times and the Third Temple are near. Imagine the sense of security and excitement you will feel knowing that world peace is imminent. Imagine the joy and well-being that you will sense on experiencing G-d's illuminating presence. Breathe in with this emotion of excitement - and out with the delicious calm feeling of trusting that everything is going to be just fine.

CHAPTER 9 - THE SOUL TRAIT OF AWE

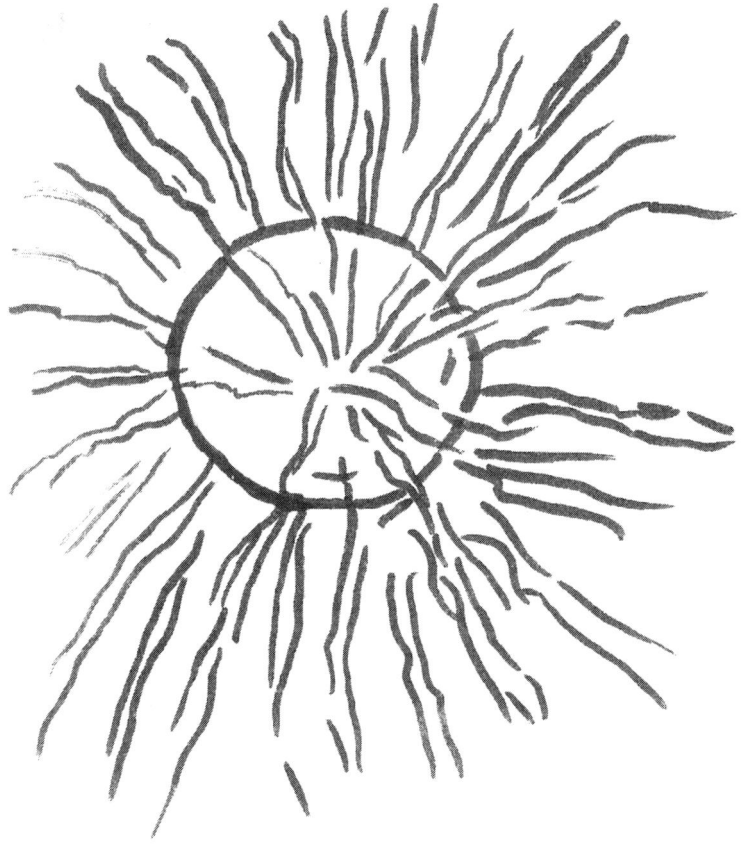

"I am continually in awe of G-d's magnificent creation"

AWE

I f I practised just one soul-trait for the sheer enjoyment of doing so - it would be that of awe.

The Hebrew word for 'awe' is *yirah* which can, in fact, be translated as both 'fear' and 'awe' – so there must be a connection between these two concepts.

On the subject of fear, sometimes we are just too scared to do anything at all - in case we make a mistake. We become too much of a perfectionist.

What, though, could be the connection between 'fear' and 'awe'? Could the acquisition of awe possibly be a cure for fear?

'Fear' or 'awe', which is more important in our connection with G-d? Rabbi Yitzchak Blazer says that the two are not equal. It is clear (he says) that 'the awe of G-d's majesty is on a more exalted plane than the fear of future accountability.'

Yet fear of G-d is still something we should reckon with. Indeed, although it is said, it is better to repent out of love for G-d than to repent out of fear of Him - surely repenting out of fear is better than not repenting at all.

Alan Morinis's view is that fear can be useful; that we should 'fear punishment for not living up to our full spiritual potential.' Maybe we could even leave out the word 'spiritual' from his statement. We all have G-d given potential to do great things in this world - and it is surely a waste of our lives if we do not live up to this gift.

Yet, perhaps Morinis has a point - if we take him to mean that we should engage with this world guided by our Jewish spirituality. And since Jewish spirituality is all about behaving in a good and godly way, then we are failing in our duty to G-d, our family and society if we act otherwise.

Rabbi Ivan Ziskind, a teacher at London's JLE, often says that there is nothing more rewarding than doing good. By not living up to our spiritual potential, therefore, we are in effect punishing ourselves.

It says in Psalms 111:10 that *the awe of G-d is the beginning of wisdom.* If so, then how do we begin to develop this most desirable of soul-traits?

One way, may I suggest, is to bask in the awareness of G-d's magnificent creation.

Alan Morinis recommends that contemplation of the beauty and wonders of nature leads to awe; yet so does focusing on the **ordinary**. We often take for granted our magnificent senses of sight, taste and hearing. Or the fact that we are, incredibly, able to walk and talk. We should occasionally meditate on these everyday marvels. We must remember, too, that the commonplace birth of a child – for instance - doesn't make it any the less miraculous or awesome….

I enthuse in Morinis's poetic language when he says:

'See the seagull and see more than the seagull. See the grass and perceive time. Look into the forest and know eternity.'

And also that of Proverbs 22:4 when it says that "On the heel of humility comes awe of the Divine."

I understand this to mean that when we recognise our smallness in this vast universe - then we become aware of G-d's greatness.

Also that if we recognise our own greatness – simply because we are children of G-d - then how much more so will we appreciate the greatness of our Creator. (For more, see Humility – Chapter Six).

And (as Morinis says) once our eyes are open to perceiving the presence of the Divine - everywhere and in everything; what moves us to pursue holiness is not fear of the retribution that will befall us as a result of wrong actions - but rather the recognition that we are living in a holy world that is a blessing and a gift. In this respect, awe triumphs over fear.

So, as an uplifting practice, let us enjoy the wonders of G-d's world - rather than get lost in the minutiae of petty squabbles.

If we need any further inspiration, we can take note of the words of Christophe Andre from his international bestseller *Mindfulness - 25 Ways to Live in the Moment through Art:*

'Ordinary objects are not ordinary, they are miraculous. Water, a glass, a coffee pot, a table, a wall, garlic bulbs - all these are miraculous. That we drink, eat, make things and belong to an intelligent, industrious, curious species is miraculous. And opening our eyes to all these unfathomable, inestimable riches that we rub shoulders with every day without (truly) seeing them is miraculous.

Of course it takes effort - a microscopic effort of presence and looking - to see all that is invisible to those who do not look. To see that we are never alone, but a hub for thousands of connections. Other human beings made this jug and this table: they found springs and built aqueducts to supply water to quench our thirst; they realised how to turn sand into glass: they grew and harvested these garlic bulbs.'

And who made man and who gave him the intelligence to do such things? The only answer for a believing Jew is G-d. How can we not have awe for the Creator of all? And when we are in awe of G-d for the magnificent world He has created, how can we possibly contemplate fear?

Contemplation leading to awe.

As with affirmations, which I refer to in Chapter Eight - Trust, visualisations (or guided contemplations) are something that I have been a fan of for aeons. Indeed I have written extensively about them in my first book *10 Days to Change your Life* as well as in subsequent books.

Alan Morinis tells us in *Climbing Jacob's Ladder* that: 'The Mussar teachers developed and appreciated guided contemplations because they understood that imagery held vividly in the mind imprints itself directly on the heart, bypassing the intellect. They recognised that we can harness the power of imagination and thought to help us on our spiritual journeying.' I would only add that the practice of visualisation can, in addition, help us to relax and to clarify and achieve our goals.

Now imagine, sitting in a beautiful place of nature. Notice the bright colours around you; feel the cooling breeze and smell the orange blossom.

Imagine touching the soft grass as you lie in the late spring sunshine. On this most perfect of days - with such beauteous weather and lush scenery - allow yourself to experience awe and wonder at G-d's marvellous creation......Take your time to enjoy its splendour.....

AWE (and Love)

Try reading the following - and internalising its meaning and power. Then recite it out loud with expression and energy.

"I am in awe of the human body. I am in awe of the magnificent natural world of mountains and lakes; hill-tops and streams.

I am in awe of the wonderful wildlife that proliferates on earth.

I am in awe of human creativity and ingenuity. The internet and television; the telephone and spacecraft; medical advances and the marvel of science.

I am in awe of the arts; inspiring music, amazing paintings, magnificent theatre, wonderful dance.

I am in awe of the love that people demonstrate and show selflessly day after day.

I am in awe of the Creator of this wonderful world.

I appreciate that humans occasionally act badly. And it sometimes seems that G-d allows too much suffering.

Yet when I see young children at play, I have an exhilarating hope that all will be well.

I understand that we are here to repair the world and ourselves; I love G-d for the continual opportunities He is giving me.

Despite the disappointments and challenges I have experienced, I am still fighting. I love myself enough to continue to strive to achieve and to give more.

I am in awe of myself – due to the amazing abilities I have been gifted by G-d.

I am in constant awe."

By adding love to awe, it is like adding energy to awe. Love is the emotion that motivates us to give, and to take action.

Love is the hidden thirteenth soul-trait. It is the additional ingredient that changes and inspires us; we just need to become aware of its presence. By adding love to any of the soul-traits, it transforms them; it powers and empowers.

I am in awe of this idea. I am in awe of G-d for letting this concept drop inside my head. I am in awe of G-d for giving us all so much amazing potential.

AWE

Waterfalls, choc-ices
Mountains - I'm struck with awe
Contemplating life's meaning
What was I placed here for?

Lions roam large prairies
Internet beams world-wide
Geysers sprout up in Iceland
Amongst them horses ride

Human bodies - quite amazing
Ears, eyes, legs, nose and brain
Clear bright colours of nature
Pure softness of fine rain

I saw a man of six foot five
A baby newly born
I'm awestruck every moment
Watching sun rise at dawn

Were you aware we only use
Ten per cent of our brain?
How long before Man reaches Mars
On cybernetic train?

Amazed by life's intangibles
Like G-d and fear and love
Fresh air, our soul, our will to live
Praise to heavens above

I'm dumbstruck by Man's power
G-d's great gifts to mankind
I'm in awe every moment
How could life be so kind?

Deserts, hill-tops and beaches
Giraffes and sun-drenched seas
Ships, planes, cars without drivers
Soon our realities

Orchestras - blue songbirds that fly
Imaginations vast
I'm in awe of your smile
Our future and our past

Winds blowing over continents…..

And every love that lasts

NUMBER NINE - AWE

One of the most amazing things in the whole of creation is you!

Is me....is man, woman, child and the whole of humankind. How can we not be in awe of *us*? A human being can talk, walk and breathe - as can other beings. Yet, it is our ability to think, create, change, and improve the world that is truly awe-inspiring.

'The word *tesha* (the Hebrew for 9) is derived from the root *sha-a,* which means *turning* or *facing.* When G-d created the world, He did not seek to create the universe in a perfected state. He intended the world to be created imperfect and that man be entrusted with the task of perfecting it. It is a call for man to perfect himself - and by extension the entire cosmos - by choosing to fulfil the Will of G-d as expressed in the Torah. In effect, G-d informs man, "Now it's your turn."

Man's role in creation - to partner with G-d and perfect the world by turning from 9 to (the perfect number) 10 - is vividly illustrated in the course of human conception. The full term of a fetus's development lasts for 9 months.'

Jewish Wisdom in the Numbers

What could be more amazing than the creation of a new-born baby? What could be more awe-inspiring than man becoming a partner with G-d? In some ways these things are minor if not major miracles.

In the last chapter, we talked about the relation between the number 8 and the festival of *Chanukah* and its associated miracles. Yet, it is in the ninth month of the Jewish year, the month of *Kislev*, when *Chanukah* occurs. So the number 9 has miraculous connotations, too.

More negatively, the number 9 is also associated with *Tisha B'Av*, the 9th of *Av* - a day on which many tragedies befell the Jewish people. For example, the outbreak of the First World War which led to both the Second World War and the Holocaust; the expulsion of the Jews from Spain in 1492; the expulsion of the Jews from England in 1290; the destruction of the two Temples which had depicted the tangible presence of G-d in the world......and many more.

The number 9 is in fact connected to the 'ultimate'. Thus, we have 'ultimate' miracles such as the *Chanukah* miracle which took place in the 9th month of the Jewish year; along with 'ultimate' tragedies that came to pass on the 9th of Av. Incidentally, it is said in our teachings, that the 'ultimate' person – the Messiah – will be born on the 9th of Av.

The messianic period will, in fact, be amongst the most awesome times in Man's history. Yet, being human, we also have to behold unbelievable tragedies with awe. We have no choice but to be shocked by them. How on earth can such terrible things have happened, we ask?

Our task is rather to **respond** in positive awe-inspiring ways; such as keeping faithful to G-d by keeping His *mitzvot* (commandments). Also to *turn toward* our fellow man and help him or her whenever we can. We do this despite - and because of - whatever tragedy (G-d forbid) has taken place.

G-d wishes us to perfect ourselves and this awesome world He has created. He has given us awe-inspiring qualities and talents. It is up to us to improve from a 9 out of 10 to a perfect 10 out of 10. Let's do it!

THE INNER SECRET OF AWE

Awe is perhaps the most wondrous of all soul traits. It is, potentially, the answer to any problem that we may encounter - at least on an emotional level.

If we are feeling depressed, for example, imagine what meditating on an immense mountain overlooking the sea (such as Table Mountain in Cape Town, South Africa) could do for us.

It is actually said in Jewish thought, that if we haven't seen all of G-d's amazing creations, then we haven't quite fulfilled our purpose in this world. I hope I've quoted that correctly, but I trust you get the gist of it anyway. There is no denying that G-d has created an absolutely beauteous world; and there is a saying in Judaism that 'the whole world was created for me.'

(The other side to this parable is that I am also 'dust and ashes.' One way to understand this is that although we have great potential and talents given to us by G-d - we are also a nothing; a mere speck in a gigantic universe - so we shouldn't get too arrogant)!

'The whole world was created for me' also means that we should both see and admire the world - as it is G-d's special gift for us. And whereas looking at a glorious painting of a majestic vista of nature may boost us emotionally, making a pilgrimage to a natural wonder such as Niagara Falls or the Dead Sea is a much more powerful experience.

Let us explore this further. I have quoted Rabbi Akiva Tatz many times before - regarding his observation that movement (of any kind) is the first step to coming out of depression. So, if we set ourselves a goal of making a journey to see one of G-d's stunning creations (and especially if we become excited by this endeavour) we are well on the way to any healing we may need.

Setting (exciting) goals is a wonderful aid to our emotional health because it leads to movement - which as we have observed is vital. *Purposeful and exciting movement*, even more so; whilst the end point of actually witnessing one of G-d's awesome creations can be literally awe-inspiring.

So awe, in different ways, can be intensely healing. But we need to take that very first step. We need to be able to summon up that very excitement and motivation - that we are looking to experience on our journey - in order to be able to start on our journey. What is the inner secret of awe that will facilitate this?

Let me first of all tell you a story of what happened to me some time ago. I had been overwhelmed by a number of things, not the least having my dear mum in hospital recovering from a knee operation. One Friday, I was rushing around like mad, especially as I wanted to be in *shul* (synagogue) in time for *kabbalat shabbat* (Sabbath prayers). Still, I am used to rushing around and struggling to be punctual!

I was around fifteen minutes behind time as the Sabbath approached. As I walked briskly to *shul*, I thought to myself: "Well at least I've done a *mitzvah* (good deed) by visiting my mum in hospital this morning. Surely G-d will forgive me for being a little late for prayers."

As I approached the gates of the *shul*, I noticed the security guard was not outside the building. This was not a problem for me as I knew the security code to open the gates. I thought that it was so late that the guard must have already gone inside. I went to hang up my coat. It had been a coldish day, but I was unsurprised to see hardly any garments in the cloakroom. Most members of the *shul* live nearer than I do - and sometimes you'll see them coming without their coats - just in their suits.

I headed for the prayer hall, and was a little puzzled to see the lights out and a seemingly empty hall. Still, very occasionally, for some reason or another, the synagogue-goers *daven* (pray) in another room in the building.

Then, suddenly, I saw the security guard.

"Where is everyone?" I blurted out.

"You're the first", he replied calmly - and I was!

I was not fifteen minutes late, I was forty five minutes early! I was astonished. In my rush to get to *shul* on time, I had totally miscalculated my timings. I was living in a parallel universe; I believed that *shul* started one hour earlier than it really did – and I was acting on that very belief.

One major insight here is **how strong our beliefs are**. If we truly believe we are going to have a good day, for instance, then everything we experience will be seen through that positive lens. We'll start to say:

"What a beautiful rainbow" (despite the pouring rain)! Or "Isn't it wonderful to be in the warm" (despite the freezing temperatures outside). Or "Isn't she a lovely person for being so kind" (even if it is part of her job to behave like that).

I believed that I was late for *shul,* so I viewed everything that happened through the lens of that (erroneous) belief.

There is a second major learning point here. In Jewish thought, it is said that G-d gives us many messages. Particularly when something happens over and over again to us, it is as if we are being sent a message - but are failing to learn from it. That is why we are given other similar situations to contend with - again and again – until we (hopefully) get the message that G-d wants us to learn.

Here, in this somewhat humorous true story, I was sent three messages. The first clue was the absent security guard. Not an obvious clue, admittedly. Although the guard normally patrols the gate, I had arrived late (so I thought) and he could well have being doing another duty inside of the building.

The second clue was the absence of coats. Now this was a stronger hint that something was up. It was a cold day. Would no-one else (besides me) have seen fit to don a winters' coat? Yet I still didn't get it.

The third clue was even more obvious. No people! OK, so it was just possible that congregants were praying somewhere else within the building, for some reason, but pretty unlikely. Still, I was so convinced that I was fifteen minutes late, that I couldn't even entertain the idea that the real time was an hour earlier than I had supposed.

We receive messages all the time, but often don't respond to them. I reacted to none of the messages in this story. Only, when the security guard (someone I felt I could trust) said to my face that I was early - very early - did I realise my mistake.

Sometimes we receive messages in dreams. Indeed, all prophets of Biblical times (except Moses) received prophecy whilst they were asleep.

We can also receive messages in other ways. If we meditate or relax our bodies enough, by tensing our muscles and relaxing them - or even just by turning off the computer - we may become inspired or sense a revelation.

Thus, the inner secret of awe - the additional boost we need to activate this wonderful soul-sense - is sleep, dreams or relaxation. For, once we are in a sufficiently relaxed or unstressed state, we are able to see things more clearly and perhaps receive messages. We will then literally be able to dream of exciting journeys, actions or goals to undertake.

This will then enable us to take that all-important first step - the movement that we need to propel us forward. This is because exciting goals have their own momentum. Looking forward to something enjoyable or fulfilling drives us forward. Did you, like me, ever awaken really early when you were much younger - because you knew you were going to get a train set for your birthday that day?

Awe is our ninth soul-trait. The ninth month of the Jewish year is *Kislev.* Its special sense is sleep and, as *Kosher Happiness* points out, is especially connected to dreams and relaxation.

The inner secret of awe is thus sleep and dreams. Dream of an exciting and worthy project and it will lift you spiritually and emotionally; enough to receive the clarity that G-d made many wondrous and beautiful creations - including that of yourself!

PSALM 127 - A PSALM INSPIRING AWE

A song of ascents of Solomon. If Hashem (G-d) will not build the house, in vain do the builders labour on it. If Hashem will not guard the city, in vain is the watchman vigilant

(Verse 1)

'(All) the energy and power that we have is an absolute gift from *Hashem.* That is what this verse tells us. Even if someone does all that is humanely possible, only with the will of *Hashem* will he be able to build a house. During a war, even if the guards keep looking in all directions, only with *Hashem's* help will they be successful in protecting the inhabitants of the city.'

Rabbi Zelig Pliskin

This truly awesome belief of Judaism is that (and I quote Rabbi Pliskin once more) 'the essential ingredient for success in any endeavour, is the will of *Hashem.*'

However, this does not mean that we must not make the effort to succeed in what needs to be done. The concept of *hishtadlus* (discussed at length in my book *Modern Day Psalms)* proclaims exactly this. Basically, we should strive to do our very best in every situation – acting as though the end result depends entirely on us. After the event, however, we must be humble and recognise that our success or failure was down solely to G-d.

Mindful visualisation for healing

The ninth month of the year, *Kislev,* corresponds to our ninth soul-trait of awe. This is the month in which the miracle of *Chanukah* took place; when a flask of pure oil – just enough for one day - lasted for a miraculous eight days. Although open miracles, such as the splitting of the Reed Sea, no longer happen - we can still see many awesome miracles in our everyday lives.

Imagine that you are the first person on earth witnessing the birth of a baby. Now visualise yourself being the first person ever to see a mighty waterfall, such as Niagara Falls. Now, see yourself as a young child discovering the amazing sprouting of a beautiful flower from the earth; or the incredible sight of a magnificent palace being built.

Now experience that exuberant feeling of joy that comes with an important prayer being answered. Let yourself breathe in and out - slowly and deeply; and as you do so, allow yourself to be awestruck by G-d's incredible creations and the precious gift of life itself.

CHAPTER 10 - THE SOUL TRAIT OF PATIENCE

"With patience I say – 'G-d wished it this way"

PATIENCE

If there is one soul-trait that we could do with in abundance – it is patience.

Let me give you an example. Behind her car wheel, Melissa begins to become agitated and impatient. "Why are the red lights on for so long? Why is the driver in front of me always so slow...?"

Meanwhile, on another side of town, Jane thinks to herself: "Why is it taking so long for me to get my act together? To marry? To find the perfect job? To regain more excitement in my Jewish spirituality?" Her list is endless; she is becoming more and more impatient.

Nevertheless, says Alan Morinis, 'there are circumstances (injustice/needs or suffering of another person; situations where our actions could make a difference) where we should not be patient and where patience is not a virtue.' In other words, we should *not* be patient at all - when we see injustice or something wrong that we can help out with.

Yet Morinis adds that we generally need 'to be able to catch our impatience as it is rising and to nip it in the bud; (that) we can choose to be patient and take responsibility for our emotional response for the situation.'

His recommendation (which he says pertains to all of the soul-traits) is that we should 'do spiritual practice NOW' - when we are not being tested; so we shall have the relevant trait to hand when we need it. His suggested practices include meditation and 'accounting of the soul'. The latter involves keeping a journal that reflects the moments in the day when one of our soul-traits is tested.

For instance, we could write: 'I crossed a traffic light, earlier today, as it was turning red. Why didn't I wait? This entry indicates that I have more work to do to improve on the soul-trait of patience. Perhaps, in future, I'll drive slower and stop at amber lights.'

Morinis reminds us that we have so little control over so many features of our lives; and by acting as if we do have control...we slip into impatience. For example, my patience was sorely tested as I attempted an early edit of this chapter. I saved my edit (which had taken nearly an hour and a half to complete) and emailed it to myself as usual. Except that I had not saved it correctly and my work was lost. So despite all my worthy efforts to ensure that the edit was done in good time – I failed. I relate this incident to remind us that we do not have mastery over events and that it is G-d who controls the world.

Working on the soul-trait of **humility** (see Chapter Six) may help. It is useful to remember how small we are in this vast universe. Focusing on this thought should assist us in contemplating on why anything should go our way. Thus, why should we get impatient when things don't?

Morinis is right to say: 'When I am good at being patient, I am living in the here and now, without straining against reality.' For me, these inspiring words describe the essence of *Mindful Judaism*.

The Hebrew word for patience is *savlanoot;* this can also mean 'tolerance' or 'suffer and endure.'

This teaches us that we should **bear** our feelings of impatience. Alan Morinis expands on this idea:

'Being patient means bearing or carrying your own emotional suffering. In practice, that means becoming aware of difficult emotions as you experience them, and then just holding them, even embracing them, so they do not take you over and dictate your behaviour.' He continues to advise 'If you anticipate that you are going to find yourself in a situation that might get heated, try to imagine in advance the argument that might take place. When your challenge arises say (to yourself) "This is what I prepared for."'

We could, for example, carry a book or magazine with us. Then, when we find that our patience is tested by a long wait, we shall be able to fill the space with a positive and enjoyable activity such as reading or reviewing some learning. Or we could simply sing or look for any humour or beauty in our situation. Patience is indeed a precious gift that enables us to make the most of the present moment.

PATIENCE (and Love)

How many times have you kicked yourself for missing an opportunity?

I have several times.

Just as we must learn to have compassion for ourselves (see Chapter Seven) so we must learn to be patient with ourselves.

If we truly love someone, we will be patient with them. If we truly love ourselves, the same will be true – as the feeling of impatience only serves to hurt us.

Moreover - patience can lead to love. Using it well will result in us being less angry - and becoming more mindful of the present moment.

Keep telling yourself (in stressful moments) "this is an opportunity for me to practise patience and to be more alive to the present moment."

Patience is a lovely soul-trait. It is so liberating. With patience, we are no longer dictated to by time - we are instead taking control over it.

You are stuck in a traffic jam. You now have the opportunity to listen to the radio, chat meaningfully to your companion or think of a creative idea. You miss a bus. You have the chance to admire the scenery or notice the people around you. Or you can use the time to practise patience.

"I still have not married again." Patience! You can choose to calmly begin anew in your search. Just as G-d re-creates the world every moment, so we have the opportunity to re-create our world daily.

I am being patient now as I await inspiration to come.

If only the Hebrews had shown a little more patience as they waited for Moses to return from Mount Sinai with the Ten Commandments, there would have been no golden calf. No wandering in the desert for forty years.

G-d exercises abundant patience with us. He forgives our sins and mistakes, not only on the holiest and happiest day of the year (which is *Yom Kippur* - the Day of Atonement) - but on other days too. We just have to ask Him for forgiveness.

We are happy, after *Yom Kippur,* because G-d has forgiven us and granted us another year of life.

G-d's patience with us thus brings joy. Our patience with others, on the other hand, may make them love us more, like us more or appreciate us more. Patience leads to peace.

Patience is an opportunity to think a new thought or to do something unplanned. It is worth its weight in gold.

Be patient with yourself and let your creative energy flow.

Love is the reward.

PATIENCE

Patience is cool
Patience is blue
It's being calm
Waiting, for you

Like a soft river
Flowing upstream
Brief chance to pause.....
Create new theme

Patience works when
Pressures a-build
Imagine peace.....
Calming green field

Lavender scent
Gold ginger snap
Think of times passed
Pre-ancient map

Patience evolves
Grand gift of time
Chance to recite
Nursery rhyme

All good things come
To those who wait
Learn not to stress
Whistle when late

Patience becomes
Woman's best friend
Love in the post
Male to send

Note with sweet smile
Giving uplift
Whence used like this
Patience's a gift!

NUMBER 10 – PATIENCE

The number 10 in Hebrew is *eser* which has the same root letters as the word *ushir* (rich); these are *Ayin, Shin, Resh*. What can we learn from this?

'The word *ushir* is synonymous with wealth; when all the physical needs of a wealthy man are provided for. In this respect, such a person can be considered to have reached a state of completion in the physical realm.'

Jewish Wisdom in the Numbers

Indeed the number 10 is very much a number of completion. There are 10 Commandments and 10 plagues. There are similarly 10 men in a *minyan;* a quorum of 10 Jewish male adults needed for communal prayer. G-d used 10 utterances in the creation of the universe.....

And when we feel complete, we stop worrying; we have inner-peace. All is right with our world; thus we find it easier to demonstrate the precious soul-trait of patience.

When we feel complete, we are able to wait more serenely in a traffic jam or at the doctor's surgery; yet this doesn't mean we need do nothing. Indeed the opposite is true. We should make the most of our 'waiting time'. We can choose to read, study, think, meditate, say a good word to someone - or, if alone, perhaps we may pray or even sing.

Yom Kippur - the Day of Atonement - is on the 10th day of the Jewish month of *Tishrei*. This is the happiest day of the Jewish year (along with the minor festival of *Tu*

B'Av) according to the *Talmud* (oral law). Despite it being a fast day, it is the holiest day in the Jewish calendar - when G-d forgives the Jewish people for their sins and mistakes.

This is what makes us so happy! G-d has incredible patience with us. He gives us chance after chance to repent and begin anew. For instance, each *Rosh Chodesh* (beginning of the new Jewish month) has an inbuilt energy of renewal for us to take advantage of.

The 10th of *Tishrei* is also the day when the Jewish people received the second set of the 10 Commandments. On the seventeenth of the month of *Tammuz,* Moses came down Mount Sinai with the first set. The Jewish people, unfortunately, miscalculated and expected him to arrive a day earlier.

They did not display enough patience. Instead of waiting a little longer, they built a golden calf. This necessitated Moses having to go up Mount Sinai again before he could finally receive the (second set of) 10 Commandments, along with G-d's forgiveness of the Jewish people.

'Olam Haba (the World to Come) was created with *yud,* the 10th letter of the Hebrew alphabet. This epoch is where the righteous glow in the radiance of the *Shechinah* (G-d's presence). This spiritual realm is permeated with holiness.

This forthcoming world also alluded to in the letter *yud* - which in the Hebrew language transfers a verb to the future tense - will be an everlasting state where the universal picture of all existence is revealed. Just as the number 10 represents the completed set, so too, in the World To Come all aspects of Creation successfully integrate into one grand tapestry that in harmony, proclaims the eternal Glory of G-d.'

Jewish Wisdom in the Numbers

It is said that *Shabbat* (the restful Jewish Sabbath) is a mere one sixtieth of the World to Come. The Jewish people celebrate this holy day with prayer, joy, learning and relaxation. Yet they have been, and still are, very patient in their waiting for the ultimate messianic time, when the world will be at peace.

Our teachings tell us that we can bring these longed-for times ever closer by doing *mitzvot* (good deeds). This is another example of how patience requires positive action to make it truly complete.

May we all merit to access this wonderful soul-trait of patience; and may be all be redeemed speedily in our days.

THE INNER SECRET OF PATIENCE

As I write this, I can already feel the surge of impatience rise within me. I feel the urge to get this section finished quickly. I'd desperately like to have this book completed, so I can move on to the excitement of teaching its practical wisdom.

Patience is a hard soul-trait to develop. It is not as glamorous as 'awe' nor as exciting as 'enthusiasm' - in fact the very word *patience* sounds a little bit boring. It has the connotation of waiting, as opposed to action. Secretly, wouldn't we much rather speed across an amber traffic light than obediently come to a stop. And wouldn't we honestly much prefer rushing in with a view of our own - instead of waiting to hear someone else's opinion? Patience can be so boring!

Yet it has many merits, too. When we are impatient to hear the result of a job interview or even a football match, this stops us being mindful and appreciating and enjoying the present moment. Now surely, attaining mindfulness makes patience a skill worth acquiring.

Patience also has a calming effect. Once we have mastered patience, we worry less. 'This too shall pass' is a famous Jewish saying. By remembering this, our stress levels will drop. Once we are patient, moreover, it is as though we are at one with ourselves – serenely accepting the ups and downs of life and behaving with total **equanimity** (see Chapter Four).

Part of the problem of acquiring patience, though, is possibly our aversion to its very name. Perhaps we should rename it and call it 'being in the present moment' or better still 'present-centred' instead. That sounds much more exciting!

Renaming it 'present-centred' or the like may well make us more inclined to master this vital soul-trait. For how we phrase something can change our attitude towards it. An important clue to succeeding in our endeavour to attain patience is the realisation that its name *is* rather boring.

Boredom is, interestingly in fact, very much connected to anger according to Rabbi Zelig Pliskin in his excellent book *Anger - The Inner Teacher.* He says that if we are irritated, frustrated or, yes, bored, these are but symptoms of anger.

This makes quite a lot of sense. For, when we are bored, it means we would rather be doing something else; and that we are probably at least a little angry or dissatisfied with ourselves for not using our time more productively or playfully.

Thus the real inner secret of patience is recognising - and then overcoming - our anger. In a way, this is ultimate *Mindful Judaism;* which is all about acceptance – yet also making the choice to be proactive and live fully in the present moment.

Yes, it is not about submission. It is about acknowledging our current circumstances and accepting our past - but it is also about being thankful for the present moment and appreciating whatever good we have in our lives right now (see Gratitude - Chapter Eleven). At the same time, it involves taking positive action and looking forward to making changes for the better.

The tenth month of the Jewish year, which corresponds to our tenth soul-trait of patience, is called *Tevet.* It is often seen as one of the more negative months of the year with no festivals and one fast day *(The 10th of Tevet)* - which is one of the four fast days in the Jewish year connected to the destruction of the holy Temple.

However, we often forget that there *is* really a festival (or, at least, part of a festival) in this month. The very first days of *Tevet* contain the end of the eight-day festival of *Chanukah,* the festival of lights, that (amongst other things) recalls when one flask of pure oil - only enough for one day - lasted for a miraculous eight days.

In this context, it may be helpful for us to think of one drop of inspired patience as being a *mitzvah* (good deed) that will miraculously last forever and ever.

The month of *Tevet* is also connected to judging things favourably (see *Kosher Happiness* for more). This brings us back to positive acceptance.

Seeing ourselves and others in a good light is a wonderful quality to have. Admittedly, accepting our current situation positively can often be challenging; but we have to remember that we can always learn and grow from any situation we find ourselves in. (See *10 Days to Change your Life* and my other books for more on this).

Thus perhaps the real inner secret of patience is overcoming our anger; by remembering that everything and everyone has a spark of good within. If we can metaphorically see this light and respond to it, our lives can yet be transformed.

The month called *Tevet* has two of the letters that make up the word *tov* which means good. If we can but **recognise the good** in any situation, we shall thence discover the mindful value of patience and enjoy the momentary space it adds to our all too often hectic lives.

'The word Tevet itself comes from tov, "good," referring to *tov ayin*, "the goodly eye" (the source of the power of blessing, as it is said: "the goodly eye shall bless"). This rectification begins with the gazing at the Chanukah candles (especially when they are complete on the eighth day).'

Rabbi Yitzchak Ginsberg (from his website inner.org)

PSALM 6 – A PSALM INSPIRING PATIENCE

Hashem (G-d), do not rebuke me in Your anger, nor chastise me in your wrath

(Verse 2)

'When we recite this verse, we ask our powerful Father and King to refrain from rebuking and chastising us, with anger. To be worthy of our request, we need to make this our own model when situations arise where we need to rebuke someone else.

As we repeat this verse, let us resolve to increase our own level of compassion (and patience). Let this compassion (and patience) come through in our choice of words and in our tone of voice. And let our own compassion, (patience) and true caring, be a model for our children, students, and anyone who observes us.'

Rabbi Zelig Pliskin

Mindful visualisation for healing

By smiling, being relaxed and saying out loud to ourselves (after a challenging time) "It was meant to be; G-d wanted it this way", we are taking to heart one of the main lessons from this chapter - as well as unlocking the door to the gift of patience.

Now visualise yourself in a frustrating or angry situation. Waiting too long at red traffic lights, for example. Notice the impatience rising up inside of you; see it as the colour red. Now imagine this hot red colour miraculously transforming into the beautiful light blue of a fine summers' sky or the bright turquoise of a calming sea.

Notice your shoulders drop and your breathing becoming deeper. Stationary, in your car, you look around and smile at a pedestrian crossing the road. You know it will soon be *Shabbat* (the Jewish Sabbath) and that you will soon be enjoying its special ambience of peace and serenity.

CHAPTER 11 - THE SOUL TRAIT OF GRATITUDE

When I express my gratitude, I am recognising the good in others and in G-d"

GRATITUDE

The Hebrew for 'gratitude' is *hakarat hatov* - which literally translates as recognising the good.

We always have something to be grateful for. At a basic, but most precious level, we have the gift of life. Also, hopefully, we have a few good friends and/or some faithful family. How about air, flowers, the gifts of sight and hearing.....? The list is endless; we just need to see and focus on the beauty and good people around us.

As Alan Morinis poetically writes: 'When you see the good in the world, it sets your heart free to soar, to shout and to sing a song of life.'

Admittedly we hear lots of bad things in the News - but then think why it is called the 'news.' It is because it's about things that are *new*, rare, and different; unusual happenings that are outside of the natural spectrum.

As well as the News, we are also continually bombarded by adverts.

Morinis wisely points out the dangers of being seduced by these. How they attempt to convince us of 'just how inadequate and lacking we are.'

"I need a new car, new glasses, updated laptop....." Well sometimes we really do - but often we don't!

Pirkei Avot (Ethics of the Fathers) Chapter 4 Verse 1 insightfully teaches an excellent perspective of gratitude:

Who is rich? He who rejoices in what he has.

Whilst Chassidic teacher Rabbi Nachman of Breslov writes:

'Gratitude rejoices in her sister joy. Gratitude doesn't much like boredom, despair and taking life for granted.'

So let's practice the attitude of gratitude to spice up our life and to give it more meaning. Let us be thankful and rejoice in whatever health, abilities and acquisitions we have.

Being a Jew (a *Yehudi)* literally defines who we are. The root of the Hebrew word *yehudi* is, in fact, connected to being grateful and thankful.

A good tip for all is to say "thank you" to every person who does even the slightest thing that is helpful or beneficial to us. Also to find something that is good in every situation - however small or commensurate that might be.

Alan Morinis warns us that advice to be happy with our portion could be mistaken for direction to be passive and unambitious, but he adds that that is simply not correct. Let us assume (he hypothesises) that we are here to be active and productive, and let us also assume we actually accomplish something that we set out to do. Without this trait of 'being happy with our portion', we wouldn't get one minute of pleasure and satisfaction from our accomplishment; we need that feeling of pleasure to motivate us to achieve more. Morinis couldn't be more correct in these assertions.

Gratitude is truly beneficial. Frumma Rosenberg-Gottlieb reminds us that 'rabbinic tradition prescribes praying three times a day, and making gratitude our first thought in the morning and last thought before sleep.' She adds that these 'established times for prayer were introduced for the well-being of the individual - certainly not because G-d needs them.'

Christophe Andre gives us further insight into the wonderful benefits of gratitude. He explains:

'Everything starts with well-being. Having a full stomach, being calm, warm and free from danger - this situation is already perfect. It's marvellous to feel like that. This elementary well-being is common to all animals, indeed to all living beings, including humans. It's possible to look no further. But this is not really happiness, because what we call happiness is much more.

If we are aware of these moments of well-being, if we say to ourselves, "I'm lucky to feel like this, it's marvellous - a grace", then something else happens. Well-being transcends into happiness. If I open my mind and savour the good things that happen to me with all my awareness, making myself present, then the impact on me of this moment will be infinitely stronger. It will go beyond the simple state of satisfied physical and psychic needs. It will be able to fulfil and calm my aspirations and metaphysical itches for meaning, belonging, love, peace and eternity...

There is no happiness without awareness. Or at best there is only retrospective happiness, as in the famous words of the writer Raymond Radiguet: "Happiness, I knew you only by the sound you made as you left." Without awareness of the present, we will long for past moments of happiness that we didn't know how to feel at the time, the stillborn happiness that we did not bring to life with our awareness.

This is what happens to us when life harries us, when we have so many things to do that we don't take time to open our eyes to all the possibilities for happiness that cross our path. It also happens when we are sad or worried. We stop living in the present and our mind remains trapped in uncertainty about the future or regrets over the past. When this happens we can only hope or weep for happiness. We can no longer feel it.'

So once we express gratitude, it denotes that we have become aware of the gifts bestowed upon us by G-d or a fellow human being. Moreover, gratitude is a soul-trait that we can get to work on right away - and on every day. Let us start by making a 'gratitude list/journal' of all the things we are thankful for - large or small.

Samantha Brick has been doing just that for the last twelve years *(Stella Magazine, Sunday Telegraph)*. She tells us:

'Even on bleak days, I'd force myself to fill in something, however simple: the blackbird singing outside, discovering a new word (when learning French), mastering a yoga move or trying out a new recipe. It has helped me navigate through some tough times, including when my TV production company folded, when I moved to France and when I discovered I wouldn't ever be a mother.

Today, I'm happier with my lot in life – more compassionate.....'

Like Samantha, we can all write out our own daily gratitude lists or keep a regular gratitude journal.

Let us be grateful for that!

I love and am thankful for the following inspiring story told by Alan Morinis at jewishpathways.com. Read it aloud and let your own sense of gratitude be enhanced.

'Rabbi Yisrael Salanter once noticed that a fancy restaurant was charging a huge price for a cup of coffee. He approached the owner and asked why the coffee was so expensive. After all, some hot water, a few coffee beans and a spoonful of sugar could not amount to more than a few cents.

The owner replied: "It is correct that for a few cents you could have coffee in your own home. But here in the restaurant, we provide exquisite decor, soft background music, professional waiters, and the finest china to serve your cup of coffee."

Rabbi Salanter's face lit up. "Oh, thank you very much! I now understand the blessing of *Shehakol* – 'All was created by His word' – which we recite before drinking water. You see, until now, when I recited this blessing, I had in mind only that I am thanking the Creator for the water that He created. Now I understand the blessing much better. 'All' includes not merely the water, but also the fresh air that we breathe while drinking the water, the beautiful world around us, the music of the birds that entertain us and exalt our spirits, each with its different voice, the charming flowers with their splendid colours and marvellous hues, the fresh breeze – for all this we have to thank God when drinking our water!"'

GRATITUDE (and Love)

"Gratitude brings one to love - and love without gratitude has no ability to endure."

Rabbi Shlomo Wolbe

By saying a blessing for the food we are about to eat - and another one for the food we have consumed - we are demonstrating our love for G-d who has generously provided us with the very sustenance we need.

By saying thank you to one and all for every service (small or large) that they have provided us - we are respecting others and adding love to their lives.

Gratitude is a blessing. It also makes us more mindful. It helps us appreciate all the good we have.

When a father blesses his children before the holy Sabbath, he is demonstrating his love for them. He is also demonstrating awareness of the blessing that G-d has given him in having children.

How can we be more appreciative and grateful towards *ourselves*, though?

The answer is simple. By working on ourselves and demonstrating good soul-traits; we will then become thankful that we are pursuing a road towards self-development and growth.

How do we make our lives longer?

By being aware and appreciative of the precious time we have. By making the most of every moment in our lives.

Jacob was asked by Pharaoh how many years he had lived.

His answer was not to give his age – but rather to relate the number of his years he felt he had lived *productively*.

We can all create good by giving of ourselves and greeting others with a smile. This is bestowing love on G-d's creatures. We can also live a more meaningful and fulfilling life by being aware and grateful for all the good there is. This is demonstrating our gratitude for the gift of life.

I was sad when my mum couldn't get around as much as she used to. Yet, I am continually inspired and grateful for how she still appreciates the good things in her life - and the way in which she offers cheery words to all she meets. Her gratitude has led to my gratitude. Who can your demonstration of gratitude inspire?

Don't take life for granted! Be grateful if you can walk, sing, smile and do *mitzvot* (good deeds). We demonstrate such gratitude each day in our morning prayers *(shacharis)* by praising G-d for our health and abilities.

Be grateful and you will live life more, love other people more - and love yourself more.

A Jew's name comes from *Yehuda* (Judah) which means to acknowledge; its root is connected to being thankful.

Gratitude leads to us becoming happier people.

It is the very secret of life itself!

GRATITUDE

Gratitude is easy
It's giving thanks to all
To G-d and human beings
Creatures both large and small

Green nature that inspires us
Pure water and fresh air
Coffee, giving a welcome boost
Brush straightening my hair

Thankful for solid table
Blank paper, trusty pen
Thanks so much for reading this
I'll write to you again!

When I awoke this morning
I saw the world anew
Appreciating sparkling eyes
Noticing colour blue…..

Lime green and red and purple
Smell of lavender wine
When practicing trait gratitude
My day turns out just fine

I don't know why G-d gave me life
What He expects of me -
Unless it's to be grateful
Unconditionally

I smiled at a girl just now
Twinkle came to her eye
Ever thankful things I do
Not knowing reason why!

I'm even grateful for those times
That seem to be bad days
Because I know the time will come
Awareness of sun's rays.....

As G-d's musician plays.

NUMBER 11 - GRATITUDE

We saw in the last chapter how the number ten is seen as a perfect and complete number. What then, is the meaning of the number 11? What can it teach us - being outside of perfection – about gratitude? We have ten fingers and ten toes, for example. What then is the relevance of this seemingly superfluous number 11 - 'outside' of normality and completeness.

'The classic personification of an "outsider" is Eisav (Esau). Just as 11 exists outside 10, the sinful twin of Yaakov (Jacob) removed himself from the spiritual set of rules that govern the universe. His refusal to subjugate himself to the Master of the Universe signalled his ill-fated decision to "step outside." There is a close affinity between Eisav and the number 11. Listing Eisav's descendants, the Torah enumerates 11 Edomite chieftains.

(Also) the gap between Eisav and Yaakov is reflected in their respective calendars. The descendants of Eisav (the Western world) use the solar calendar of circa 365 days; the Jewish calendar principally follows the standard lunar year of 354 days. That means there is an 11 day difference between them (in a non-leap year).

The succession from 10 to 11 (thus) resembles the journey from "completion" to "unnecessary excess." These two numbers beautifully encapsulate the respective diverging worldviews of Yaakov and Eisav.

Yaakov declared *Yaish Li Col* "I have everything". His search for spirituality meant that he would wholeheartedly use all of his possessions in the service of G-d. Everything was essential; nothing was extraneous. This explains why Yaakov risked his life to retrieve several significant utensils. *(Talmud commentary on Parshah Vayishlach).*

This sharply contrasts with Eisav's outlook. His determination to grab "more and more" meant a never-ending accumulation of wealth, well beyond his essential physical needs. His proud boast *Yaish Li Rav* "I have much" declared an obsession with more possessions than he would ever need. His pursuit of addiction indicates an ideological failing, one that would interfere with the pursuit of perfection.'

Jewish Wisdom in the Numbers

Thus the number 11 helps teach us that the trait of gratitude – being thankful *for all we have* (as opposed to an obsessive wanting of "more and more") - is a wonderful asset in our quest for happiness and inner peace.

THE INNER SECRET OF GRATITUDE

Today I had reason to be grateful.

It's funny how things work out. A few months ago, I picked up a friend at a bus stop outside a local tube station. That was where my problems started! A couple of weeks later I received a surprise letter through the post telling me that I had broken the law by 'parking' at a bus stop. I had been spotted by a speed/traffic camera and was landed with a fine. I made a formal appeal to the local council. I had inconvenienced no-one and there was not a bus to be seen!

However, I knew this would not wash with the council. I made my main grounds for appeal, therefore, that they had not put the correct address of the contravention on the notice. I thought my best hope would be to get off on a technicality. The council, nonetheless, rejected my objections. So, I further appealed, as was my right, to an independent tribunal.

Take two. Two weeks further on, I was shocked to receive yet another PCN (Penalty Charge Notice) from the same council. Apparently I had turned right into a 'no right turn' road. I was certain they had made a mistake, so I revisited the scene of the alleged crime. Sure enough, there was a 'no right turn' sign that I had totally missed. I don't know why it was there and I had caused no problem – but again a traffic camera (this time a secret one) had spotted me. I had made a genuine mistake but I was in the wrong.

However, I was annoyed at the council for using a hidden traffic camera and suspected that it was there primarily as a means of extorting monies from the public. Hardly grounds for an appeal, though. Nevertheless, I had a hope; the council had printed the address incorrectly again! There was a big letter 'o' overtyped on the word 'Drive' making it read like 'Driog' instead. So, once more I chose to exercise my rights and go to an independent tribunal.

I went to the first tribunal hearing. When the judge realised that my main reason for appeal (incorrectly addressed PCN) was the same for both cases - and that the very same council was involved - the case was adjourned. It was put back by three weeks in order to be heard at the same time as the second appeal. Today, I went to the tribunal again. Both cases were heard and the tribunal, believe it or not, found in my favour. Victory! No fines. I had every reason to be cheerful and very grateful, thank G-d.

Sometimes, it is obvious when to feel gratitude. Today was one of those moments. However, the truth is that we should be grateful every day; several times a day. Grateful for when we are in good health. Grateful when we have successfully relieved ourselves in the toilet. Grateful for our family; our friends; the bus driver; our car; the fact that we can walk, breathe, sing, speak. The list is endless – which is why Judaism encourages us to say blessings; over a hundred a day, I believe.

Yet, we often say these blessings by rote and forget to really *feel* grateful. What then is the inner secret of gratitude - one that will bring this valuable quality into our hearts?

Gratitude is the eleventh of our soul-traits and thus corresponds to the eleventh month of the Jewish year, *Shevat*. According to the *Sefer Yetzirah* (the oldest book in *Kabbalah*) the special sense of this month is 'correct eating.' This brings us back to the idea of saying *barachot* (blessings) – in this case over food. It is a wonderful thing to do. But, as we have said above, there is the danger of saying any blessing parrot fashion. Why should blessings over food be any different?

The difference with food is that we say **two** blessings when we eat; one before we partake and one afterwards. The first blessing offers a marvellous opportunity to be mindful. That of taking a moment before we eat - rather than stuffing the food into our mouths straightaway, without really savouring and appreciating it.

By truly enjoying our food in this mindful way, we are in a much better position to thank G-d *afterwards* with a second (after)-blessing; for providing us not only with the sustenance that we require - but also with a culinary delight. For G-d could have created the world so that our sustenance comes in the form of pills or capsules instead. Much less appetising!

Of course, we should also be thankful that we have sufficient money to buy the food. Also, grateful to anyone who has helped make the food; or who has sold or delivered it to us.

When we express our gratitude, we should be recognising not only the kindness of G-d for providing our sustenance - but also the good of others for their part in the process of bringing the appetising food to our dinner tables.

If we really wish to connect to this amazing soul-trait of gratitude, saying blessings over our food and eating mindfully are great ways to start. Eating is the inner secret of gratitude.

PSALM 104 – A PSALM INSPIRING GRATITUDE

How abundant are Your works, Hashem (G-d); with wisdom You made them all. The earth is full of Your possessions

(Verse 14)

'Every cell in our body is complex, all the more so the trillions of cells that make up each human being, working together in magnificent harmony. (Then) there is the universe with all of its galaxies and suns and planets. The oceans and seas and all of the fascinating creatures that call them their home. The world of birds, physics, chemistry, mathematics are all manifestations of *Hashem's* infinite wisdom. Understanding even a small part of the world creates within us a tremendous sense of fascination and awe. Some people feel this with more intensity and others with less, but anyone who spends time thinking about this, will have a greater sense of appreciation for the wisdom of the Creator.'

Rabbi Zelig Pliskin

This is just a small part of what we mean when we say "The whole world was created for me" or as Louis Armstrong once sung, "What a wonderful world!"

How can we not be thankful for all the magnificence that G-d has provided us with?

Mindful visualisation for healing

Some things are easy to be grateful for. A beautiful spring day. A marvellous sunset. The bus approaching a moment after we arrive at the bus stop…..

The eleventh month of the year, *Shevat* - that corresponds to our eleventh soul-trait of gratitude - contains the festival of *Tu Bishvat*, the New Year for Trees. This occurs either in January or February, depending on the vagaries of the lunar-solar Jewish calendar. Yet, whenever it falls, nature always seems to display its indications of the upcoming spring at this time. It is thus easy to feel grateful and optimistic on this day; with its signs that winter is about to end – and that warmer weather will thankfully soon be on its way.

However, it can take more effort to appreciate other more everyday things - which is why we Jews are encouraged to say blessings. These help us become aware of the good all around us and enhance our lives immeasurably.

Visualise yourself awakening in the morning, both excited and grateful for the new day ahead. You are thankful to G-d for giving you yet another day of life – so you say a heartfelt blessing. You relieve yourself in the toilet and say a blessing of thanks for being able to do so. You then enjoy a glass of cool, fresh orange juice and say a blessing both beforehand and afterwards.

You walk to the station and are thankful for the light wind and fresh air that you are able to breathe. You then take a bus and think how grateful you are to the bus driver - and to those who constructed the vehicle; enabling you to travel safely and efficiently.

You are thankful for the woman sitting opposite who gives you a cheery smile. As you notice a beautiful tree through the window, you mentally proclaim thanks to G-d for His wonderful creation of the world.

At work, you confront a challenging situation and are grateful to G-d for providing you with the abilities to deal with it.

On your way home that evening, the weather is freezing - but you are thankful for the protection of your warm coat and sturdy shoes. You imagine yourself on a beautiful beach shaded by palm trees. Then you awake - and think to yourself what a gift it is to have such a vivid imagination. You laugh at a joke you hear. Isn't it wonderful to be alive!

CHAPTER 12 - THE SOUL TRAIT OF SIMPLICITY

"I accept and enjoy what is simply now"

SIMPLICITY

In the end Kohelet (Ecclesiastes) finds meaning in simple things. Sweet is the sleep of a labouring man. Enjoy life with the woman you love. Eat, drink and enjoy the sun.

That ultimately is the meaning of *Succot* as a whole. It is a festival of simple things. It is, Jewishly, the time we come closer to nature than any other, sitting in a hut with only leaves for a roof, and taking in our hands the unprocessed fruits and foliage of the palm branch, the citron, twigs of myrtle and leaves of willow.

It is a time when we briefly liberate ourselves from the sophisticated pleasures of the city and the processed artefacts of a technological age and recapture some of the innocence we had when we were young, when the world still had the radiance of wonder.

We are all strangers on earth, temporary residents in G-d's almost eternal universe. And whether or not we are capable of pleasure, whether or not we have found happiness, nonetheless we can still feel joy.'

Rabbi (Lord) Sacks

If the soul-trait of simplicity ever sounds a little boring - don't despair. It is, in fact, exactly the opposite as we can see from the above praise of simple things. Our final soul-trait of simplicity, simply leads to joy!

Alan Morinis affirms this, telling us that the plain-sounding 'soul-trait of simplicity does not have its own chapter in *Orchot Tzaddikim (The Ways of the Righteous)* but where that trait is discussed is within the "Gate of Joy."'

How can that be, we may ask? To investigate, let us consider its connection with gratitude (see Chapter Eleven) - in that simplicity, like gratitude, entails being content with our portion – that has been gifted and tailored specifically for us, by G-d.

When we are content with what we have, our heart bubbles with joy. Wanting more than what we have is not wrong - indeed we rightly need to be ambitious; but letting our desires frustrate or incapacitate us in any way goes against enjoying the *simple* pure pleasures of everyday life.

What do we really need in our lives? The truth is that we can gain joy from the everyday - such as a simple walk or the blessed relief in recovering from an illness. From a lovely summers' day; especially that fresh and satisfying feeling (in England) after the rains have departed. Or from a friendly and welcoming smile. Give one to someone!

On *Shabbat* (The Jewish Sabbath) we have time to engage ourselves in simple things; to study, pray, meditate and walk; visit friends, rest, review texts studied and much more besides.

The busy preparation for the day has become worthwhile; for now the Sabbath has arrived, we have the opportunity to experience pure and simple joy. We are granted the precious gift of time.

Without a TV, radio, cell-phone or laptop to distract, we can focus on enjoying the simple things around of us. Without needing to acquire anything new on this most holy of days, we can enjoy happily living in the present.

This doesn't mean that (on other days) we shouldn't buy new things. Indeed, I, personally, gain much joy from acquiring a much-loved CD by Al Stewart, Dusty

Springfield or the Zombies, for example. Or an art book by Edward Hopper or the French Impressionists.

Still we must learn to appreciate the simple things in life too – that don't require money. We can start by enjoying our current acquisitions. I love re-discovering old books that have been lying unopened for aeons, for instance.

Yet, as my earlier books point out, the Jewish festival of Passover *(Pesach)* teaches us that there is also a time for us to clear out and spring-clean - so we don't get too cluttered up.

As *Pirke Avot* (Ethics of the Fathers) 2:7 states:

'The more possessions, the more worries'

Christopher Andre eloquently explains:

'Our society of multiple forms of abundance also creates multiple deficiencies within us, and the two are linked. Think of diseases of excess, for example, those modern maladies of *too much* - too much food that makes us obese, too many possessions that make us morose. Too much of something is always a lack of something else, and excess always generates deficiency.

We know, for example, that industrially produced, refined, aseptic foods are not only unhealthy because they are 'too much' - too present, too accessible, too sweet, too stimulating to our appetites leading to diabetes and obesity - but also because they have 'not enough' of many vitamins and minerals. Contemporary deficiencies also apply to our psychic needs, such as the need for calm, slowness and continuity. We must strive to ensure that we obtain these in order to stop ourselves falling ill (from stress, emotional instability and mental fragmentation).

Combatting a lack of slowness means taking our time; not flitting from one activity to the next, not doing several things at once. Instead we must act calmly and gently whenever possible; restoring ourselves with a dose of doing nothing, drawing on the healing powers of simplicity, calm and one activity at a time. We must unplug.

As an act of freedom, we can just close our eyes and stop watching the screens that steal our attention, constantly eating into our brain time and moments of rest.'

I, personally, thank G-d for *Shabbat* (the Jewish Sabbath) and the Jewish festivals that, when properly observed, provide us with technology-free days. Without *Shabbat* and the festivals, it would become very difficult for us to withdraw from such activities voluntarily - even for a short time.

On a psychological level, simplicity means letting go of the past and accepting (and enjoying) what is now. (Of course we must still learn from the past – just not get imprisoned or incapacitated by it).

As Alan Morinis points out:

'Being content means accepting that you have been allotted; everything you need for the present, according to a wisdom that is higher than anything your human mind can access.'

In other words, G-d knows better than any one of us what we truly need for our growth - and what we require to achieve our purpose in life.

This discussion brings us back to **trust in G-d** (see Chapter Eight).

Simple trust leads to joy. Sometimes life is simpler than we think.....

Rabbi Akiva Tatz (in *Letters to a Buddhist Jew*) expounds on the meaning of joy for us:

'*Real joy is what you experience when you are doing what you should be doing.* Joy is the *neshama's* (soul's) response to doing what it should be doing. Our vision of joy has nothing to do with forgetfulness or the ignoring of suffering; it has far more to do with the mature appreciation of a life developing correctly.

When you are moving clearly along your unique path to your unique destination, you experience real joy. When you are moving along the path that leads to *yourself*, to the deep discovery of who you are; when you are building the essence of your own being, expressing your destiny in the world, *creating yourself and making your contribution to the broader reality,* a deep happiness wells up. The journey does not cause joy - *the joy is the journey itself.*

You cannot feel depressed when you know you are moving correctly towards a correct goal. You may feel pain, you may feel agony; your face may show strain and your eyes may fill with tears; but if you are winning the battle and moving ahead, you cannot be *depressed.*

Often it is necessary to start the movement externally: getting the body moving may be necessary before the soul can be roused. Judaism teaches that the "external awakens the internal;" experiences and actions of the body stimulate inner experience.

Whether the activity is vigorous body exercise or exacting work for the hands (or best of all, active work in giving, doing something to benefit someone else) the principle is to convert stagnation into action.

One who is labouring to build and is aware that the result is taking shape as it should, *cannot be depressed* no matter how hard the work.

I must point out that there is an alternative to depression as a response to lack of life movement, and it is perhaps even more dangerous. It is possible to satisfy the deep need to build by building trivial things. This escape can provide…..a result which is *enough to keep a person from the real task* of life - without the warning sign of a sense of emptiness or depression.

People will build collections of objects or throw themselves into projects that are meaningless because the total commitment and extreme, focused effort give a sense of purpose and movement; the fact that the purpose is irrelevant or foolish is easily ignored.

Some people build collections of paintings, some build collections of beer cans. Some devote themselves to sporting achievement, some to business. Some build muscle, some build empires. All of these have the potential to appease the urge to produce, to move, to build; at least for a while, and sometimes for a lifetime.

But very often they are simply superficial substitutes for the real work of building the self and the world correctly. Building things in this world may be necessary and worthy, but when the building here becomes a substitute for the building of eternity, that is a tragedy.'

Building ourselves, practising self-development and working on our soul-traits will surely bring us the most reward.

One day at a time: it's that simple.

SIMPLICITY (and Love)

The more we are grateful for things (see Gratitude – Chapter Eleven) the more mindful we become - and the easier it is to practise simplicity.
By being grateful for our possessions, we can then ask ourselves honestly how many of them we actually need. Those we don't, we can either give or throw away.

Having less can sometimes lead to us appreciating more.

Have you noticed how children can be deliriously happy and engaged with a basic colouring book or a cheap bouncy ball?

I remember awaiting a wind up train set for my seventh or eighth birthday. I was so full of joy.

Simple is good; especially when we become grateful and mindful. What joy there is feeling a fresh breeze on a hot summer's day; or noticing bright stars on a clear frosty night. And is there anything better than a cool glass of water - when we are desperately thirsty?

I was in Hong Kong once when the skies opened and the rain bucketed down. There was absolutely no point in me trying to stay dry. So what did I do? I started jumping deliriously in the puddles. Simple really; I engaged with the reality of a potentially unpleasant situation - and transformed it into pleasure. What fun!

Accepting our situation with equanimity (see Chapter Four) is a simple solution to dealing with the ups and downs of life. Of course, we should strive to do well and improve our lot. Yet, what is more satisfying than making the most of the present moment?

If you find yourself alone, why not meditate, think out of the box or do something creative?

The simplest solution to life, though, is to **love** the current moment and engage in it positively.

Yes we can plunge our thoughts into negativity - into the bad things happening in our lives or that of others. And if we are in physical or emotional pain, it is truly not easy for us. But if, when we can, we discover love and give to another - whether it be money or time or a smile – our lives will gradually improve.

It is as simple as that. Love G-d, love the moment, love others and love yourself. Simple!

SIMPLICITY

Playing piano – one by one single note
Learning to recite rhythmic poem by rote
Answering questions - sometime yes, sometime no
Observing blowy waves; westward winds come and go

Sporting coloured shorts, delightful summer's day
Watching young children inventing child's play
Embracing *Shabbat*, it's so pleasing to me
Ending *Yom Kippur* fast, soothing cup of tea

LIFE'S SO FULL OF JOY…..GRACED WITH SIMPLICITY

Chatting with dear partner, tube, bus, ship or plane
Puzzling Sudoku sharpening frazzled brain
Stroking old cat Thomas, helping faithful friends
Hoping cherished time, lovely mum, never ends

Giving praises to G-d, much overdue thanks
Noticing coloured fish, swish-swaying, deep tanks
Taking mindful stroll, rest under dappled tree
Thank-you card for all; creating poetry

LIFE'S SO FULL OF JOY…..GRACED WITH SIMPLICITY

Loving caring family…..special shared harmony……

LIFE'S SO FULL OF JOY…..GRACED WITH SIMPLICITY

NUMBER TWELVE - SIMPLICITY

You may wonder why I have chosen 12 primary soul-traits to explore in this book (along with the additional all-encompassing trait of *love* that permeates each chapter).

The number 12 is a simple and natural number. We can see this clearly – there being 12 months in a normal year (although thirteen comprise a Jewish leap year). There are similarly twenty-four (two times 12) hours in each day. Plus there are the 12 Tribes of Israel – let's learn more:

'Everything within existence in the lower realm reflects a higher spiritual concept. There are 12 permutations of the ineffable 4-Letter Name of G-d *(yud kay vov kay)*, which represent the pathways of Divine influence in the universe.

The foremost vehicle is through the *Shevatim,* 12 Tribes of Israel, in whose merit the universe stands. They are parallel to the 12 pillars that uphold the world. Indeed, all of G-d's workings in This World (as overtly manifest in 12 hours and 12 months) correspond to the 12 Tribes. Yaakov's 12 sons are responsible for giving the natural world a meaningful structure within which to interact.

In actuality, the first human being, Adam, should have himself fathered 12 sons. But his primeval sin meant the designation *Israel,* in the mission to glorify G-d through 12 pathways in This World, would not be given to all of mankind.

Instead it would be reserved for the chosen descendants of Avraham (the Jewish people).......Finally it was left to Yaakov (to father the 12 tribes).'
Jewish Wisdom in the Numbers

It is said that Adam sinned because he wanted to know the difference between good and evil - for a holy purpose. He felt that (his eating from the tree) would give him both the knowledge and the *choice* to choose good; thus G-d would be pleased with his exalted service.

However, as we see, his attempt to second-guess G-d failed miserably. G-d had commanded him not to eat from the Tree of Knowledge of Good and Evil. It was a simple instruction that Adam sought to complicate – and it led to him experiencing death rather than remaining immortal. (*aish.com*)

I heard something similar from Rabbi Akiva Tatz. King David asked G-d why he wasn't held in the same high esteem as Avraham, Yitzchak and Yaakov. G-d said it was because He had tested the other three and that they had passed their tests. David then said to G-d, "So test me too." However, once he had said this, he had failed his test! The moral being that we should not request additional tests and challenges in life from G-d, however noble our aims are.

In both of the above instances, the simple way was ignored – that of following G-d's commandments.

Staying with the moment is normally preferable than seeking complication. Enjoying a few moments in the sunshine; talking to someone you love; saying a kind word to someone. Smiling.....

The 12th month of the Jewish year (that corresponds to our 12th soul-trait of simplicity) is the month of *Adar* - which contains the festival of Purim. This exhilarating festival is so joyful and yet it is based on simplicity. People dress in costume or simply wear a mask or hat. Small food gifts are exchanged. A joyous, fun-filled s*euda* (meal) that normally contains wine and meats takes place. *Tsadakah* (charity) is given to all who ask. This doesn't actually have to be much. The main principle being that we try to give something; that we are all here to help each other - without judgement or prejudice.

Sometimes *Purim buskers* will knock on our door and, if invited in, will sing, play music or entertain – to raise monies for a worthy cause.

In addition, a simple yet wonderful story is told about a King (Ahasuerus), a villain (Haman) and two Jewish heroes (Mordechai and Queen Esther). The festival is comprised of simple happenings and commandments - and yet, when observed in full, becomes so meaningful and joyous.

When faced with a difficult decision, we should inquire of ourselves what we truly value. When involved in an argument with a loved one, we should ask ourselves what's really important; winning the argument or maintaining a good relationship? Often, a simple pertinent question can aid clarity and point us in the right direction.

Children are wonderful examples of simplicity. They can be so full of joy with an ice-cream (or two!); try watching them playing with a small toy – or with a real or imaginary friend.

Laughter is the special Kabbalistic sense of this 12th month of *Adar* (see my book *Kosher Happiness*). Yet laughter is not just a gift of children, it is for us all to enjoy. Laughter is natural. It is only when our soul becomes tainted or covered with dross that it becomes harder to access. When we become more holy by doing *mitzvot* (commandments and good deeds) we will find that we can connect more with our soul and laugh more easily.

Children, in particular, seem to be able to enjoy all 12 months of the year. They make the most of their summer holidays; ride a bike (or play conkers) in autumn; build a snowman in winter and roll down hills in the spring.

The natural order of the world can be seen in the Number 12. One two (1 2) enumerates 12! What could be simpler?

Simplicity simply leads to joy.

THE INNER SECRET OF SIMPLICITY

Oh, for a life less complicated! A rabbi I know recently asked me how I was. "Busy", I replied diplomatically. "Busy, that's good" he responded. But is it?

Sometimes, there is so much going on, so much to do. It can be hard enough for us to take care of ourselves; so looking after a friend or relative, for example, can often be a major challenge. In life, there is often a plethora of things we *need* to deal with, as well as many other things that we would *like* to do.

How can we make life more simplistic, then? One day at a time, has to be the mantra. It is interesting that the Jewish day starts at dusk. This reminds us that preparing for the day ahead is best done the night before. Packing our bag and writing a 'to do' list the night beforehand - are two simple acts that can make us feel well-prepared to confront and enjoy the next day's challenges.

"One day at a time" is mindful. It helps us not to become too overwhelmed. I'm sure we'll have plenty of things to deal with in a month from now, a week hence - and even in two days' time. But they must wait, if only for the sake of our own sanity. Yes, we can plan for the future - and reminisce or ponder over the past - but the most important day is *today*. One day at a time is the simplest strategy.

Yet what is it that will help facilitate and deepen this approach? What is the true inner secret of simplicity - that will enhance our practice of it? For our twelfth and final soul trait, we need to look at the twelfth Jewish month of the year, *Adar*, for guidance. That month's special sense (according to Kabbalah) is 'laughter' which brings to mind the famous saying 'G-d laughs whilst man plans.'

This points us towards the wonderful festival in *Adar* - that is *Purim* - when Haman's evil plans for the Jews were turned on their head and the Jews were eventually saved. There is much merrymaking and laughter on *Purim*.

It is also notable that our forefather Isaac's Hebrew name is *Yitzchak*, whose root is laughter. Avraham and Sara were aged one hundred and ninety respectively when Isaac was born. Sara laughed on learning they were to have a son at such advanced ages.

The truth is, that we simply don't know what's going to happen in life. We don't even know for certain what the weather will be like in a few days time - let alone the state of the world. 'G-d laughs whilst man plans' and yet perhaps we would be better off saying 'G-d plans, so man might as well laugh!'

The simplest thing to do, therefore, is not to worry (admittedly easier said than done) and laugh instead. We are being mindful when we accept and enjoy what is simply now.

Life is simpler than we think, especially if we follow the Jewish way of thinking. Jewish law commands us, for example, to visit the sick, honour our parents, escort the dead and comfort their relatives. Apart from such general obligations, that we all have, we each have a unique contribution to make too. In fact, as we saw earlier on in this chapter, Rabbi Akiva Tatz tells us that we find joy when we do what we were created to do.

Thus, it is wise to observe Jewish law (in general) and to follow our life-mission - according to our own individual skill-set and talents – in particular. We must try our best, as though everything depends on us; yet, after the event, we should say "it was all down to G-d."

This, in essence, is the secret of laughter. We laugh when the unexpected happens. The typical clown tripping on a banana skin is, in a way, a cruel joke. Yet its psychology is that we laugh because the act was unexpected and came out of the blue. In the same vein, we should be able to laugh at ourselves and our lives - because **we are not really in control**. G-d plans, so man might as well laugh.

It is as simple as that. Things may or may not turn out as we expect. Thus, we should be laughing all the time. It is G-d who controls the world - not us. We saw it with the unexpected birth of Isaac and with the deliverance of the Jews on *Purim*. We see it when a millionaire loses all his money or a pauper becomes a prince.

This is my fifth book. Unbelievable! How did it happen? Even if it was somewhat down to my unique skill-set, who was it who determined my abilities? G-d. Sure I wanted to write a book, but how many others say they'd also like to write one, but don't? It is G-d who engineers the circumstances that allow our successes to happen. We can only put in the effort and pray for our wished-for result to materialise.

We must thus learn to laugh at life and not to take things too seriously. Start by watching a comedy film, or enjoy some cartoons; or laugh along with a child - just to get yourself going. Laughter is a serious matter. It gives much value to our lives and others and is the very key to living life more simply and productively. And simplicity, as we saw earlier on in this chapter, is in the gate of joy.

The inner secret of simplicity is thus laughter. Learn to laugh. Practise laughing. Simply laugh!

PSALM 150 – A PSALM INSPIRING SIMPLICITY

Let all souls praise Hashem (G-d)

(Verse 6)

'The *Midrash* (deep teaching) from *Yalkut Shimoni* comments on this verse, the last verse of Psalms: "Praise Hashem for each and every breath." The Hebrew word for soul is *neshamah,* similar to the word *neshimah,* breath.

This is a strikingly fitting way to conclude *Tehillim* (Psalms). We have much to be grateful for. And the gift of being able to breathe oxygen is the biggest gift of them all. Breathing oxygen is life giving. Without fresh oxygen one cannot exist. With each breath you take, you are inhaling the fuel necessary to keep you alive right now.'

Rabbi Zelig Pliskin

It really is as simple as that. G-d has gifted us a soul and the means to breathe, thank G-d; and it is up to us, in return, to follow His commandments and to study His wonderful guide book to life - the *Torah.*

Of course, as this very book you are reading points out, we must also strive to become holy by working to improve our character and soul-traits. By doing so, we will truly be able to love (and behave kindly towards) our neighbour for the benefit of all concerned.

Mindful visualisation for healing

The twelfth of our soul-traits, simplicity, corresponds to the twelfth month of the Jewish year, *Adar*. This is the month which contains the fun and joyful festival of *Purim*.

This festival is both mindful and simple. Amongst other things, we enjoy a festive meal and give charity to the poor. The latter we do without even thinking to question motives. Just the fact that someone needs to ask us for assistance is a good enough reason (on *Purim*) to respond positively.

On this special festival, we also give simple gifts of food to our friends; preferably through *shaliachs* (messengers); these are often children. The optimum way of giving charity is to give it anonymously. This ensures that we avoid getting too proud of our 'worthy' act.

Lastly, we hear the complex yet simple (almost) fairy-tale about the wicked Haman, the blessed Mordechai, the beautiful Queen Esther and the buffoon of a king, Ahasuerus.

We also, like the simple man, get drunk – preferably on wine. (This is to fulfil the commandment of not being able to tell the difference between the blessed Haman and the wicked Mordechai – or is it the other way round)!

Now visualise yourself enjoying the beautiful simple pleasures of Jewish life. Firstly imagine yourself sitting at a Passover *Seder* table (hungry!) taking your first bite of *matzah* (unleavened bread) for nearly a year.

Suddenly, you are transported into a *succah* (outside hut) and are waving a *lulav* (palm branch) together with some myrtle, willow and an *esrog* (citron); right and left, up and down, forwards and backwards; symbolising that G-d's presence is everywhere.

Now winter arrives and you see yourself mindfully lighting eight coloured *chanukah* candles. Then it is *Purim* and you are dressed in a fancy hat and funny costume.

Finally, it is an ordinary non-festive week, but the Sabbath has arrived and you are clothed in your *Shabbat* (Sabbath) finery; eating and drinking the tastiest food and drink in heart-warming company.

Then you go for a simple walk in the park; noticing and enjoying G-d's glorious creation of nature…..

WHY DOES A LOVING AND ALL-POWERFUL G-D LET BAD THINGS HAPPEN TO GOOD PEOPLE?

This is a question that has often disturbed and perplexed me. For in Jewish thought, we are meant to believe in an all-powerful and loving G-d.

If this is a correct assumption, though, then why would He want or allow the righteous to suffer? Why isn't this world a much happier place? Why do some people die young? In fact, why must anyone die at all?

I have often been puzzled and bothered by these questions.

The nearest I had come to an answer was that G-d 'punishes' or rather rebukes people in order to give them a wake-up call - so that they will mend their ways and become better people. This seemed both palatable and plausible; but I couldn't understand, nonetheless, why G-d couldn't just give us a gentle reminder - such as a light cold or a missed bus; rather than disease, destruction and death - in order to prompt us to do better.

In January, 2017, Rabbi Yitzchak Schochet gave a presentation (in three parts) at Edgware's Lubavitch Synagogue on 'Do bad things happen to good people?' I use these classes as a basis (together with my own considered thoughts and opinions) to try to come to some sort of an answer to one of the most perplexing questions of all.

Rabbi Schochet intoned, first of all, that if we take G-d out of this equation then there *are* no questions. If we claim that G-d doesn't exist, then our question (about G-d allowing bad things to happen) disappears; it is just a matter of survival of the fittest.

It is our belief in G-d that makes the hardships we see prick at our conscience. Just to be able to ask the title question to this piece, we have to believe in G-d – and a loving and all-powerful G-d at that.

If we posit that G-d is not all-powerful, then the question would have to be, "why does *Man* do bad things to good/innocent people?" If, on the other hand we believe G-d to be all-powerful but not loving, we have our answer straight away. It would be that He doesn't love or care about humankind, therefore, He punishes us or lets us be hurt (G-d forbid).

Thus this question can only meaningfully apply if we believe in a loving and all-powerful G-d. That therefore must be our starting point - if we truly wish to engage with this issue.

So why *does* a loving and all-powerful G-d allow bad things to happen to good people?

In his class, Rabbi Schochet encouraged us to look at this matter from G-d's perspective – which fits in with another discussion I heard on the same topic by Rabbi David Katz.

From G-d's perspective, he said, we have to wonder whether we are actually 'good' people after all. For sure, none of us are perfect; not even our greatest prophet Moses – who was not quite deserving enough to be allowed to enter the land of Israel.

Moreover, it goes without saying that we all 'sin' - if we use the Hebrew word for sin, *chet*, in its literal way. *Chet* means to miss the mark - as an archer may do when aiming at a bullseye.

We all 'miss the mark' to a greater or lesser extent and G-d, especially when we call Him by the name *Elohim* acts from a place of strict justice. Yet G-d is often called *Hashem* too, a name which denotes His attribute of mercy.

Why, then, shouldn't He be merciful towards us? It is G-d who created mankind as imperfect – so why would He blame and punish us when we *behave* imperfectly? OK, so He also gave us free choice to do good (as well as bad) and, according to Jewish thought - and the famed eighteenth century rabbinic scholar the *Vilna Gaon* - we should all strive to be 'the best person we can be.'

Yet, if we do sometimes 'miss the mark', as we undoubtedly will – do we really deserve to be punished by G-d with death, hardship, illness or troubles?

Going back to Moshe (Moses); he wanted to know more about G-d, so he asked him what His name was.

Names are very powerful in Judaism. The Hebrew word for name *shem* is connected to *neshama* which means soul – thus our name describes the very essence of who we are.

G-d replies to Moses: "I shall be as I shall be". This cryptic response left G-d's essence and His modus operandi regarding suffering (or anything else for that matter) hidden from Moshe.

Similarly when Yaacov (Jacob) was in battle with a heavenly angel, he asked the angel for its name. The angel replied, "Why are you asking my name?" Again, the secrets of heaven were concealed from a holy ancestor.

The point is that we are not meant to know the reasons for everything that happens.

Sometimes we just have to say "I don't know."

Rabbi Schochet made the case that there are different types of not knowing. The "I don't know" of a child, for instance, can be qualitatively different from the "I don't know" of a scientist who has examined all available evidence. "I don't know" is thus a valid answer to the question of why there is suffering; especially when it comes from a place of deep examination into the subject.

Also, if we knew one hundred per cent why the innocent suffer, would we still feel compassion for them? If we were truly aware of why G-d 'punished' someone, there would actually be no need for us to feel sorry for them. We would simply accept G-d's decision as just.

Another possible answer is connected to that of free will. Our ability to weigh up a decision and to make a choice is one that is intrinsic to human beings. However, if people have the free will to do good then they also have free will to commit evil. This, unfortunately for us, allows suffering to take place.

Yet cannot G-d prevent or alleviate some of that suffering? And what about the suffering caused by nature? Tsunamis, floods, earthquakes, natural disasters.......They are nothing to do with Man's free will. Why does G-d not step in and cancel them (or their effects) out?

The former Chief Rabbi, Lord Sacks, when asked why there was a tsunami, replied that the question should not be why – but rather **what** can we do to help? What would G-d want us, as decent human beings, to do in such a situation?

Despite this, we can and should express upset; that is what any good human would do. Yet, we must also continue to maintain our faith. (Quoting from Rabbi Schochet) we should say: "In spite of You (G-d), I am going to carry on believing in you."

In the *Ashrei* prayer (Psalm 145) that we recite three times daily, we state "You open your hand and satisfy the desire of every living thing."

This can be taken to mean that G-d only gives us what we need – and what we can deal with. Thus everything that we encounter in life is tailored especially for us and our particular capabilities.

G-d knows that we can handle the specific challenges that He has given us. They may, in fact (according to Rabbi Schochet) bring out a latent potential – and our response may make us magnificent!

To be sure, we may not be able to handle *another* person's problems and tests – but they are not meant for us. For others, we can only feel and express compassion - and try to help out as best we can.

Rabbi Schochet quoted from his own father when he was close to dying. I can only paraphrase, but the essence of what he said was that "the sign of true trust (in G-d) is continuous joy." This may sound simplistic, but as we learned in Chapter Twelve – simplicity is in the gate of joy.

Whatever is happening in the world around us, or in our own personal lives, there will still be moments to celebrate such as *simchas* - joyous occasions like weddings and *Bar Mitzvahs*. There will also be, particularly when we are being mindful, wonderful moments of nature to contemplate and acts of loving-kindness to observe. We can, in fact, create our own happiness – by noticing the good and by doing good - if only we have the will to do so.

Thus the best answer as to why G-d allows bad things to happen to good people, might, in fact, be the most simple one i.e. "I don't know."

Our optimum response, though, must be to give a helping hand where we can - and to express compassion.

For our own challenges in life, the best spiritual response is to improve on our character and soul-traits; to become the best person we can be – and to serve G-d with joy. For without inner joy, we will simply be unable to serve G-d and humanity in a truly meaningful way.

MINDFUL POEMS FOR HEALING CONTEMPLATION

'I have my books
And my poetry to protect me'

Paul Simon (from the song 'I am a Rock')

The benefits of poetry and the Psalms can be immense - as is detailed in my books *Poetry for Health* and *Modern Day Psalms*. Whenever we have to face anxiety or stress, I encourage taking solace in King David's Psalms; either by reading them to ourselves or reciting them aloud.

Similar advantages can also materialise when we read relevant poetry in a mindful way; absorbing their meaning and rhythm. In that spirit, I include, here, a few poems for you to try on for size. But don't forget to read King David's majestic *Tehillim* (Psalms) too.

I hope you will enjoy the following eight poems that I have composed and that they - along with the suggested *Mindful Thoughts* following them - will provide you with spiritual food for both meaningful and mindful contemplation.

TRANSFORMATION (Déjà vu)

It's not quite déjà vu
A bird flies into view
Into deserted coloured sleeping-room

I'm back here at Ascent
Where many hours spent
Transformation to blue light - no more dark gloom

It always is a time of self-discovery
When insights fly in like an un-caged bird
Never failing to bring road to sweet recovery
From something I have seen or maybe heard

This time I met a non-Jew who was wondering
A girl who changed her hair five times a day
Amidst it all sounded lightening and thundering
Yet still I struggled through it all to pray

I experienced several acts of loving-kindnesses
Never knowing whether best to laugh or weep
One secret I learned - Show your open-mindedness
Don't judge - With faith, allow yourself to leap

It's not quite déjà vu
Though she enabled me to write
Poem inspired by *Safed*
Just like this very night

Group could have been this one
Different faces yet same souls
Each searching through their art
Each playing their own roles

I met a rabbi, sung own composition
Young girl most beauteous I've ever seen
All searching through their lives - healing condition
Trying to figure out what it all means

How could that man once believe false religion?
Then transform into an observant Jew
Bird swooping surely must have been a pigeon
Noah's ark and sacred Temples once she flew

I'm wondering who she is and what she knew.....
I'm wondering where you are - and who are you

Mindful Thought

I wrote this poem in kabbalistic Ascent in wonderful mystical *Safed* in Northern Israel; a place well-worth making a pilgrimage to. It was based on my experiences of a particular visit in early 2016.

Try relaxing and getting mindful when reading this meditational poem; focusing particularly on the lines:

It always is a time of self-discovery
When insights fly in like an un-caged bird

FRENCH LAMENT

"Now we'll all sing *La Marseillaise*
To show that terror never pays
Now we'll all sing *La Marseillaise*
Trying to live out normal days"

Paris is bombed by ISIL
Stabbings on Israel's streets
Anniversaire of Mumbai
History repeats

Europe labels 'West Bank' goods
Teachers pontificate
In England's universities
It's Israel they hate

"Now we'll all sing *La Marseillaise*
To show that terror never pays"

At school I studied *Le Français*
I've read the Little Prince
Travelled to France when I was young
And loved her ever since

Yet now its streets I fear to tread
Champs Elysees, I'll go back?
Guitars playing *Montmartre*.....now
Music's under attack

"Now we'll all sing *La Marseillaise*
Trying to live out normal days"

And what of dear old Blighty
How safe in London's rain?
Will you or I take Eurostar
Journey to France's pain?

Whilst Cameron and Obama
Choose leave our lives to fate
Making disgruntled noises.....
Yet always hesitate

"We have policies on Iran
That's not enough to please?
They want to nuke your Israel?
Our stance is to appease"

Same when it comes to ISIL
Britain sits on its hands
"It's parliament who must decide"
Cameron reprimands

He speaks in French to *Les Français*
His way to create bond
Yet may wait till England's attacked
Before tries to respond

(He says):

"Now we'll all sing *La Marseillaise*
To show that terror never pays"

When I was young, I loved French films
Jane Birkin, Je t'adore
Will I visit *chere France* again
Feel safe on England's shore?

One day, perhaps, we'll take account
Of Israel's just views
Alone, she knows, world peace starts with
Protection for all Jews

It's action that is needed
Not sitting on our hands
Nice words alone won't win this war
Will England understand?

"Now we'll all sing *La Marseillaise*
To show that terror never pays

Now we'll all sing *La Marseillaise*
Trying to live out normal days"

Mindful Thought

This poem has become even more meaningful since I wrote it in November of 2015. Last week, on Wednesday 22nd March (2017), a British-born terrorist (convert to Islam) murdered innocent civilians by driving into them on Westminster Bridge in London. He also stabbed a policeman to death.

Events like this have been going on in Israel – and latterly in Europe too – as *French Lament* depicts. The world looks on but, particularly in regards to Israel, often turns the other cheek. That is until it affects **them**. When will the world learn that the enemies of Israel are also the enemies of mankind?

This poem was written after the Paris attacks of November 2015 and a shortened version of it was published in England's *Jewish News*. Unfortunately, its message appears to be timeless.

It is important to be aware that being mindful, in a Jewish way, also entails remembering and learning from our individual and collective past. It is nearly the fifteenth of *Nissan*, *Pesach* (Passover) as I write – a time when we are commanded to remember our freedom from Egypt. It is worth focusing on the value of remembering - by meditating both on the above poem and the following:

'Twelfth-Century master, Maimonides, writes that "On the night of the fifteenth of *Nissan* it is a positive command of the Torah to relate the miracles and wonders that transpired with our forefathers in Egypt, for it is written: 'Remember this day on which you went out of Egypt,' [and the meaning of 'remember' here is] similar to that which is written 'Remember the day of Shabbat."

Why does the Rambam (Maimonides) find it necessary to liken the manner in which we remember the Exodus to the way in which we remember the Shabbat? Why doesn't the verse "Remember this day on which you went out of Egypt" stand alone?

At the beginning of the laws of Shabbat the Rambam states: "Resting from labour on the seventh day is a positive command, for it is written, 'On the seventh day you shall rest.' Whoever performs labour at that time negates a positive command and transgresses a prohibitive commandment."

Thus Shabbat involves both the positive aspect of rest and the negative aspect of not performing labour.

The fact that the Rambam begins the laws of Shabbat with the positive command, notwithstanding the fact that most of the laws of Shabbat deal with prohibitions of various forms of labour, indicates that the main aspect of Shabbat observance lies in this positive aspect…..

Thus, the more important part of "Remembering the day of Shabbat" is the positive sense of rest rather than the mere negation of labour, as our Sages state that after the completion of the Six Days of Creation the world was lacking rest and tranquillity.

Only when Shabbat began did rest and tranquillity arrive. Or as the Rambam expresses it: " 'Remember it' - a remembrance of praise and sanctification."

With regard to the exodus from Egypt as well, we find two aspects: the release of the Jewish people from servitude, and the fact that we became a free, independent people.

This is similar to the condition achieved by every freed slave: His master's dominion over him ceases; as a free man he becomes wholly his own person.

By connecting the tale of the Exodus on the fifteenth of *Nissan* to remembrance of the Shabbat, the Rambam is indicating that with regard to relating the events of the

Exodus too, the main aspect is the positive step of becoming free.

For just as remembering the Shabbat involves not so much the negation of labour as the positive theme of rest, so too the obligation to relate the tale of the Exodus involves not so much the recalling of our release from slavery as the recounting of how we became free men.

Thus the Rambam goes on to say in the following law that even when one relates the tale of the Exodus to a son who is a minor or simpleton he should say: "On this night G-d redeemed us and took us out to freedom," thereby emphasizing that G-d enabled us to become free.

Consequently, the Rambam goes on to say that "An individual is obligated to conduct himself as if he himself had just gone out of Egypt" - "as if you yourself were enslaved, and you went out to freedom and were redeemed."

One should conduct himself on this night as a free man.'

Adapted from the works of the Lubavitcher Rebbe, Rabbi Menachem M. Schneerson, of righteous memory. (Likkutei Sichos, Vol. XXI, pp. 68-73.)

Let us all take some time to remember and learn from our individual and collective past; may we all be truly free.

BEGINNING

Today I'm starting a new chapter in my life!

I'm smiling at each person that I meet.....

Little boy that once was me
In dusty photo case
Winning in athletics class
Old-time school running race

Baby playing on the floor
In high-chair being fed.....
Yerushalyim's cool air
Under G-d's *Chupa*, wed

Loving; how I used to love
A skill I knew so well
Football in ancient playground
Playing kiss-chase and tell!

Tuneful music of my youth
Still floats around my mind
Smiles from loving grand-parents
Always so good and kind

Running for the bus one day
My grandma nearly slipped
Just like my old-time memories
Times recalled, others skipped

I sometimes sit and wonder
What purpose is it all?
Perhaps I should just shrug and laugh
Answer G-d's siren call

Mindful Thought

Here we look at memory once again.

Let us relax our bodies; and, particularly focusing on the last verse - contemplate what it is G-d wants from us.

TIME (Messianic)

If we magic'd more time
No rushing around
Skies always would blue
Sun lighting our sound

Roses smelling wet scent
Smiles - all those we'd meet
Time purring with glee
All beings we'd greet

Messiah's on his way!
World peace breaking out
Kids dancing in streets
Romancing with shouts

I'm in tune with G-d's world
Dream's now coming true
Living for all time
Life-loving anew

You know, nearly forgot
How time likes to wait
Swings soft in the park
Moments celebrate

Seconds jump up and clown
Play cello on train
Love fellow once more
When true king comes reign

Every day filled with joy
All wishing to serve
Each other and G-d
Man's losing reserve

So we'll pray arrives soon
Blessed day of the king
Just needs one more act
That our smiles will bring

Let's forget too much tact.....
Bare our souls, share and sing!

Mindful Thought

If we magic'd more time
No rushing around
Skies always would blue
Sun lighting our sound

STUDY TO *KIPPUR*

"Why aren't you more like me?
Why don't you want to see?
I'm also part of you
It's me who's the real Jew

I like to learn
To read wise books
I'm not concerned
With how one looks

In fact although
I love to read…
It's not at all
My Jewish creed

Caring what one
Wears on his head
It's learning that
Counts when you're dead!

Not cap nor *tallis*

Nor black hat

It's deeds and study

Where it's at!"

"I'd like to answer if I may
Life - not death - must have its say
Each *kippur, tallis,* cap or hat
Is truly where our lives are at!

They show the world just who we are
Affecting all those near and far
Dressing the part - clothes make the man
Help us become part of the clan

Wear *kippur, tallis,* cap or hat
Then world will know where your life's at
People shall see you as a Jew
You thus become one – And me too!"

Mindful Thought

This poem has an enigmatic title – but, as with any puzzle, once you know the answer it makes perfect sense.

What we have here is a conversation between two Jewish ideals. Our first protagonist is (or speaks up for) the worthy value of Jewish learning and study. The second extols the virtues of Jewish dress and identity.

Which one do you prefer to give priority to?

Or maybe both?

NOW!

It's time, dear G-d, for me to write
'Cause think you've made an oversight
Although so much you've given me -
I lack peace, calm and harmony

Feel all alone, without a bride
Who'll give me help, stand by my side
With little baby on her knee -
Happiness, joy and love thence be

As days increase, become more old
Emotions cease, I get less bold
Ideas don't come, no more can do
Except rely solely on You

Wonders occurred at the Reed Sea
When Israelites at last came free
All that I ask, something as good
If You so wished.....I know You could

What point is there if I'm alone?
Which punishment must I atone?
Much better that You make new start
By putting love in one girl's heart

So that she'll wish to marry me
Provide us both with family
Sweet girl I'd dare ask be my wife
Completing me, sharing my life

Don't know what else there is to say
'Cept thank You for gifts of today…..
No good for man to be alone:
Please make that call on heaven's phone

Asking good woman be my wife
Such tiny act would change my life
We'd build a Kosher home with love
Our deeds would light heaven above

So please, dear G-d, don't hesitate
Let me meet up with my soul mate
Thence happiness we canst create…..
Happiness wilt create

Mindful Thought

This is a poem which is truly a Modern-Day Psalm (see my book *Modern Day Psalms*) – a simple honest prayer from Man to G-d.

What is its message?

That we should keep sharing our hopes, wishes, troubles and concerns with G-d. A problem shared is a problem halved; and it is just possible that G-d may answer us in the way we wish.

If not, then we must keep praying, asking - and taking action best we can – knowing that G-d is always listening and has our best interests at heart.

Although we are not at a level to understand G-d completely (even Moses wasn't) we must continue to have faith that everything is for the best. (See more in Chapter One - Faith).

THE BALLAD OF SHARONA S

Mysterious Sharona S
About her one can only guess
I met her once as if by chance
Led me one right merry old dance!

She puzzles, Miss Sharona S
Or maybe Mrs, who can guess?
When kindly deigned give me her email
I thought "what a friendly FEMALE!"

Thus contacted dearest Sharona
Asking whether she mind I phone her
Yet took my request with dismay
(saying) "Mail is my choice today"

So mailed I, her, many questions
Praying she'd offer faint suggestions
Re who she was, what she enjoyed
In case I could fill any VOID!

That she may have in secret life:
I didn't ask her be my wife!
Yet must now say, if canst digress
That I quite liked Sharona S

I hoped, at least, she'd be my friend
Knowing, on me, she could depend
So waited for her to reveal
Something about her that was REAL!

Humans are surely made to share
And for each other deeply care
Sharona, though, refused to say
What was on complex mind that day

(said) "These questions I sure don't need
I'd prefer a good book to read"
Then shook me up when sudden said
"Our conversation is now DEAD!"

You'd like to know where Miss S lives
If she's the type always forgives?
What food she likes, what's in her mind
Jewish girl, caring, good and kind?

How tall she is - and what's her age?
And now transgender's all the rage
Whether ever was born a man.....
Or for Prime Minister she RAN!

She hinted she once felt some grief
Behaviour? "Beyond belief!"
Mail address? It came from France
Sharona led me merry dance

So if you ever meet Miss S
Please don't expect her answer "Yes"
'S' stands for secret, don't you know?
She'll act all friendly, then say "NO!"

As soon as you dare ask a question.....

(Let offer me, just one suggestion
If you seek woman to impress
Make sure it's not Sharona S)

And if you'd like someone to phone ya
Don't hold your breath for my Sharona
You'll never ever get to know her.....

She's really not worth all the pain
About herself, she'll ne'er explain

I'd like to see her once AGAIN!

Mindful Thought

To be Jewish sometimes requires a sense of humour.

As expressed more than once in this book, we really can't be expected to understand all of G-d's ways. G-d, our creator, is infinite whilst we are mere mortals. Thus, when we are faced with puzzling behaviour or an odd happening, our best response is to laugh and get on with life.

We can remind ourselves of this by reading the above poem with a smile on our face. The mysterious Miss S is a good example of someone whose behaviour is impossible to understand. Instead of crying over her refusal to grant us what we want – we should become mindful, move on and simply chuckle at her oddball ways!

COUNTRY FOLKS

Love the trees
Cool fresh air
Country living's in my hair

Guitars playing
Voices sweet
Girl-a-swaying
At my feet

Butterflies
Light of moon
Joy knowing I'll see her soon

Children chasing
Just for fun
Adults facing
Glimpsing sun

Love the views
Love your jokes
Run through puddles, clothing soaks

We've become country folks

Now we all are country folks!

Mindful Thought

A lilting poem to lift our spirits.

Perfect to contemplate and meditate on when working on the soul-trait of simplicity (see Chapter Twelve).

After-Word - How to have a Mindful Year

I write this on the fifth *Tishrei* (25th September 2017) just after *Rosh Hashana,* the Jewish New Year.

In our New Year prayers, we recite:

Hashem melech - G-d reigns – (Present)
Hashem molach - G-d reigned – (Past)
Hashem yimloch - G-d will reign – (Future)

Similarly, on *Rosh Hashana,* we focus on three major themes - in the following order:

Malchiot - G-d's kingship – (Present)
Zichronot - Remembrances – (Past)
Shofarot - Signifying future redemption – (Future)

Without going into too much detail, I would like to suggest a commonality here. In both cases there seems to be, firstly, a focus on the present; then the past; and lastly on the future.

This is obvious in our first example: *G-d reigns, G-d reigned, G-d will reign.*

In our second illustration, we can see clearly that remembrances are about the past. Also, that G-d's kingship - very much *the* theme of the day - is very much present tense; as on *Rosh Hashana* our primary focus is on coronating (and relating to) G-d as our king and ruler.

Shofarot, on the other hand, has varying connotations; one of its major ones being the **future** arrival of the Messiah.

The point I'd like to bring out here is that whereas we normally think in a linear fashion i.e. past (followed by) present (followed by) future - on *Rosh Hashana,* we (as indicated above) seem to place stress on the **present** before the past and the future.

Why should that be?

From a Mindful perspective, we know it is the present that should be our main focus - whatever concerns we may have about our past or future.

From a Jewish point of view, *Rosh Hashana* is the day(s) when we are judged for who we are *at that present moment.* So, it is then that we should have in mind the ideal person we truly aspire to be.

We have plenty of time – after *Rosh Hashana* – to work on the practical details of achieving this. (I first heard this idea from Rabbi David Roberts of Kehillas Netzach Yisroel).

Rosh Hashana is also, like all beginnings, the seed of our future actions (a topic that is a favourite of Rabbi Akiva Tatz). As the popular saying goes: 'You never get a second chance to make a first impression.'

Thus, *Rosh Hashana* informs us of the importance of staying in the present moment. The festival also incorporates the first two days of the *Ten Days of Penitence* which culminate in the Day of Atonement that is *Yom Kippur.*

Both festivals are, in fact, intrinsically connected. They are referred to collectively as the *High Holy Days.* Indeed, it is said that our judgement for the next year - which takes place on *Rosh Hashana* - is sealed on *Yom Kippur*. The implication being that we still have time to sweeten this judgement by showing good intentions and behaviour in the period leading up to *Yom Kippur*.

Moreover, on *Yom Kippur* itself, by demonstrating genuine repentance and by returning to more godlike ways - it is remarkably said that we can actually transform our sins into *mitzvot* (good deeds).

How exactly can this be done?

As previously discussed in this book, the word for sin, *chet,* literally means 'to miss the mark.'

One common 'missing of the mark' occurs when we focus too much on our real or perceived missed opportunities of the past.

Yom Kippur teaches us how to deal with these.

On this festival, we are specifically encouraged to confess our sins verbally *(vidui)* as well as regretting having committed them and resolving not to do them again.

Relating to this in a mindful way, we can see the benefits of doing this.

By saying out loud (for example): "I messed up my relationships - with people, G-d and even myself" or "I really didn't achieve my potential this past year; I wasted a lot of time doing inconsequential things" - we actually stop mulling over our past failures by bringing them into the open and making them more tangible.

We can then visualise the person we'd truly like to be. (This was actually our *Rosh Hashana* work).

This process clears our minds wonderfully and instils energy into our intention to improve ourselves in the coming year.

Thus, by being mindful - by saying aloud our mistakes now IN THE CURRENT MOMENT - we release our past sins or mistakes and allow them to be replaced with new positive intentions; these will hopefully lead to good actions and behaviours *(mitzvot)* in the coming year.

By being and focusing on the present, we can thus use our past to bring about a promising future. Remember:

Hashem melech (G-d rules) - Present
Hashem molach (G-d ruled) - Past
Hashemi yimloch (G-d will rule) - Future

I wish you many blessings for the future as you practise *Mindful Judaism* with joy.

PREVIOUS BOOKS BY MARVIN J SHAW

Modern Day Psalms: How to Connect with G-d and Ourselves in the 21st Century

Poetry for Health: The Power of Poetry to Heal and Fulfil

Kosher Happiness: A 12 Step Programme to Reveal and Release your Inner Potential

10 Days to Change your Life – The Ultimate Jewish Self-Help Book

To contact Marvin, please email him at:

tendaystochangeyourlife@hotmail.com